135 Gunstock

CARVING PATTERNS

135 Gunstock

CARVING PATTERNS

Lora S. Irish

Fox Chapel
PUBLISHING

ISBN 978-1-56523-795-7

Cover and page 2 art by Bill Janney.

Library of Congress Cataloging-in-Publication Data

Irish, Lora S.
135 gunstock carving patterns / Lora S. Irish.
pages cm
Includes index.
Summary: "Create one-of-a-kind functional artwork that will be cherished for years to come with this treasury of classic gunstock carving patterns. You're sure to find the best carving pattern here for your next project. From basic checkering to dramatic relief carved scenes, nationally recognized carving artist Lora S. Irish presents 135 great gunstock patterns featuring traditional sportsman and hunting-related themes. She offers an array of excellent choices for every skill level, from beginner to expert, so you can start with a basic pattern and tackle more intricate designs as your experience in gunstock carving grows. The patterns in this book are designed for rifle stocks, but are just as applicable for knife handles, pistol grips, or duck calls. And while these patterns are specifically designed to be relief carved with hand tools, they are equally usable with power carving tools, woodburners, laser engravers, and sand blasters. Patterns include animals like deer, elk, moose, bears, mountain goats, and puma, plus birds and waterfowl such as quail, pheasant, ducks, geese, eagles, and more. Designs are provided for panels, ornaments, banners, scrolls, oak leaves, fishscale, basketweave, and checkering. The author offers advice on choosing patterns, wood, tools, and carving methods, plus tips on whether to start from scratch or use a kit"-- Provided by publisher.
ISBN 978-1-56523-795-7 (pbk.)
1. Wood-carving--Patterns. 2. Gunstocks. I. Title. II. Title: One hundred thirty-five gunstock carving patterns. III. Title: One hundred and thirty-five gunstock carving patterns.
TT199.7.I743 2013
736'.4--dc23

2013007000

To learn more about the other great books from Fox Chapel Publishing, or to find a retailer near you, call toll-free 800-457-9112 or visit us at *www.FoxChapelPublishing.com*.

We are always looking for talented authors. To submit an idea, please send a brief inquiry to acquisitions@foxchapelpublishing.com.

Printed in China
Second printing

Contents

6 About Gunstock Carving

Part 1

7 Gunstock Carving Basics

8 Working with Patterns
10 Getting Started
12 Wood Choices
14 Tool Choices
16 Finishing

Part 2

17 Gunstock Carving Patterns

18 Animal Patterns
33 Bird and Waterfowl Patterns
38 Eagle and Scroll Patterns
51 Butt End Patterns
54 Panel Patterns
77 Checkering Blueprints
92 Stock Templates

95 Index

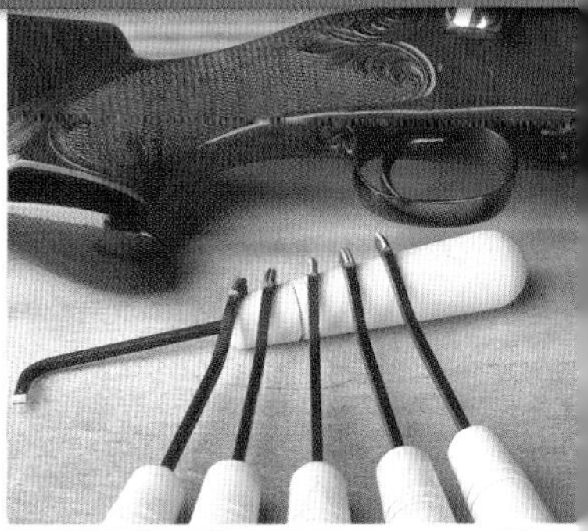

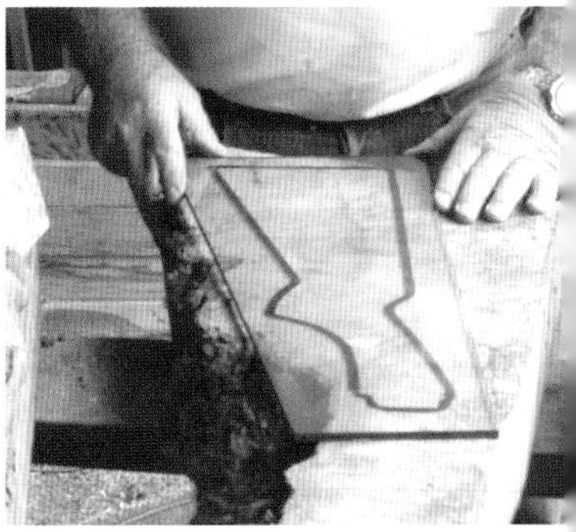

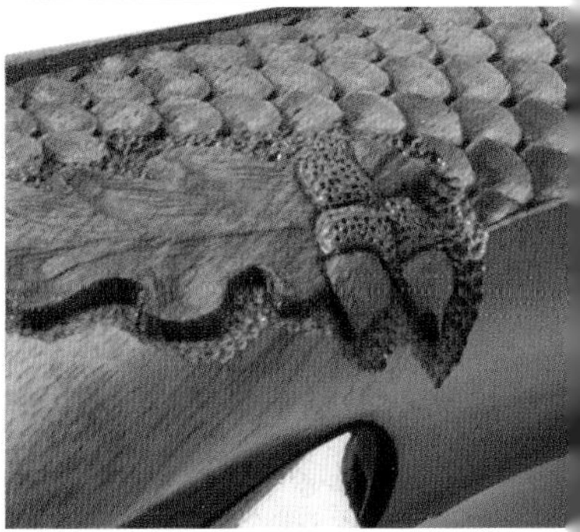

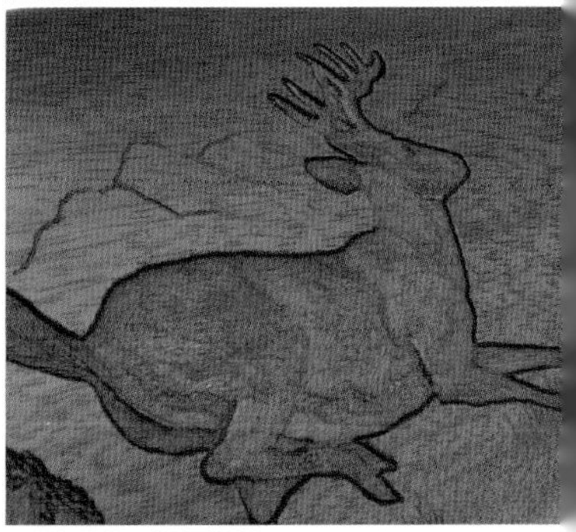

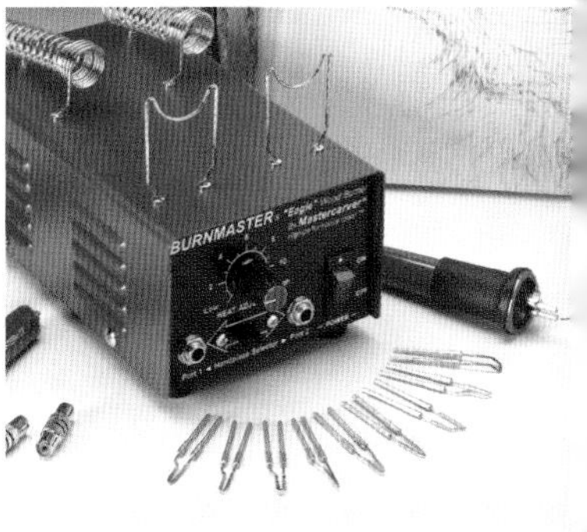

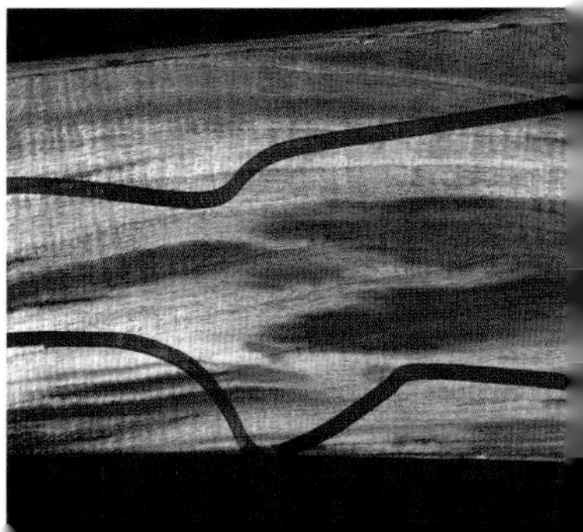

About Gunstock Carving

Lora S. Irish's strongest memory of her father's gun carvings and restorations is a smell—a strong, pungent smell that permeated the house and made her wrinkle her nose when she went downstairs for breakfast in the morning.

One of his first restorations started while Lora was waiting for her mother to make her purchase at a yarn store housed in an old barn. Her father noticed an old rifle resting in the rafters. When he questioned the shop owner, she told him that her grandfather had owned the gun but it had misfired, leaving a live bullet in the chamber. On her grandfather's death, her grandmother, afraid of the rifle, put it in the rafters. Lora's father asked if he could have it so he could restore the rifle to its original condition.

The restoration process took months. Her father had to disassemble the weapon (after unloading it), clean the dirty rusty pieces (hence the horrible smell from the steel pieces soaking in bluing and browning solutions), and then search for replacements for any missing pieces. He then did a close evaluation of the stock. Was it worth cleaning up? Or should it be replaced completely?

Lora S. Irish

From that first project, Lora watched her father restore many guns. Some were straightforward restoration projects that just involved disassembling, cleaning, and reassembling the pieces; other projects required that he carve a new gunstock. The designs he used, basic checkering patterns and relief carved scenes based on hunting-related themes, are the inspiration for this book.

PART 1

Gunstock Carving Basics

A hand-carved gunstock can add both beauty and value to a firearm—if done correctly. As you consider using the patterns in this book for your next project, keep these two guidelines in mind.

1. Know your skill level
2. Know the gun's purpose

Knowing your true skill level—not the level you aspire to be—is a factor in every step of gunstock carving. Are you a beginner, intermediate, advanced, or expert carver? The honest answer to that question is your key to success in everything from choosing a pattern to picking which wood to use to deciding whether to start from scratch or to use a kit.

Knowing the gun's purpose is equally important. Is this a display-only item? Will it be used in the field? What type of hunting will be done with it? Your answers will help you decide which pattern best fits the gun you are carving.

Take the time to answer these questions so you will have a clear idea of your skill level and the gun's purpose before you move forward with choosing a pattern, wood, and a carving method.

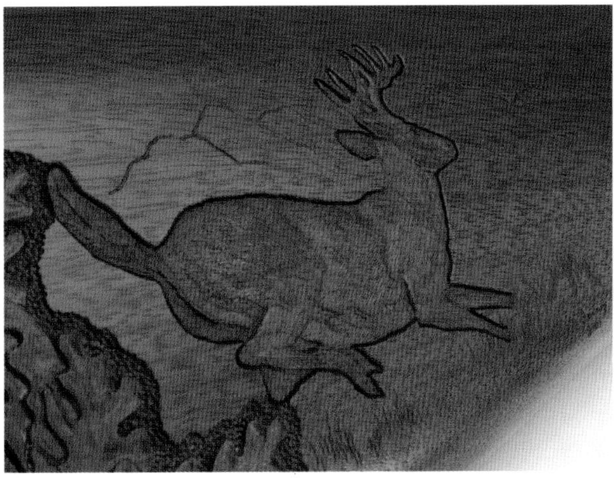

Many gunstock patterns, including the ones in this book, are meant to be relief carved with hand tools. Relief carving gives the finished piece a rounded, dimensional look, because the background of the carving is lowered, allowing the central image to stand out. Relief carvings done in large thick pieces of wood can have a great deal of depth and dimension, like the mule deer shown at the left. Gunstock relief carvings can be carved to a depth of about ¼" (0.5cm), creating a shallow relief carving like that shown in the gunstock at the right.

Working with Patterns

With your skill level in mind, take a look through the patterns in this book. Choose one that you *know* you can do well, not one that you *might* be able to do well. Even a simple, well-executed pattern or motif will enhance the personal and monetary value of a gun with a hand-carved stock. When you're sitting with tools in hand and gunstock at the ready is not the time to see if you're up to a challenge. As your experience in gunstock carving grows, you will soon be ready to tackle those harder or more intricate designs.

Of the patterns you choose, which fits the purpose of the gun? Common sense dictates that you don't want to carve a water scene with a duck on a rifle that will be used for deer hunting. But your considerations should go much deeper than just matching what is portrayed in the scene with the type of hunting that will be done. You'll also need to consider if this rifle will be used in the field or if it is for display only. If the gun is still in use, pick a pattern that enhances the hunter's grip but doesn't interfere with the cheek rest.

Altering a pattern

Any of the patterns in this book can be altered to fit your skill level. If you are a beginner, consider deleting elements or simplifying lines to make the pattern fit your confidence level. Experienced woodcarvers may want to enhance a pattern by adding more elements or including more detailing on the figures.

Many options are available for altering a pattern. For those who like to work by hand, a common way is to place a light table under the pattern and then combine or enhance elements by copying them to tracing paper. By making printed copies of several different patterns, you can cut out areas of each to create an entirely new design. For those who like to work with computers, try using a drawing program to alter scanned images.

Utilizing the Patterns

The patterns in this book are not limited to gunstocks. They can be resized to fit a number of different hunting items, including duck calls and knife handles. These small surfaces provide an excellent canvas for checkering designs or simple patterns.

PHOTO COURTESY OF BILL JANNEY

The patterns in this book can be used for any hunting-related item. These duck calls, carved with dental power tools by Bill Janney, are just one example.

Sizing a pattern

Any pattern you choose will need to be sized to fit not only the length and width of your gunstock, but also the curve of your gunstock. Patterns in this book can be sized in two ways: distortion or reduction/enlargement.

Distortion, which refers to stretching an image by either length alone or width alone, can be used easily with patterns that feature borders. Simply cut the borders into pieces, tape the pieces to the gunstock, and then extend the lines to make the border fit the area you want to carve. For example, to size a pattern that features a duck inside borders, cut out the duck, distort the borders as explained above, then tape the duck in place inside the borders.

Certain elements, including some animals and leaves, can be distorted and still appear attractive. The spread wings of an eagle, for example, can easily be stretched outward to more evenly fill an empty space.

Other animals and elements need to be reduced or enlarged as a whole by changing the width and the length to the same proportions. A photocopier or scanner can make this process easier. Carvers who prefer to draw by hand often use a grid system to ensure the correct proportions of an enlargement or a reduction.

Gunstocks curve in two directions—from the butt to the grip and from the top to the bottom—so patterns need to be clipped, or eased, to fit the curve of a gunstock. Tiny straight cuts or small V-shaped darts will help the pattern lie flat against the wood. You may need to fill in some areas with freehand drawing to keep the integrity of the pattern.

Transfer the pattern to the stock by slipping a piece of carbon paper, face down, between the pattern and the wood. You might also choose to glue a closely trimmed pattern directly to the wood.

Not every pattern must fill the full space available or be surrounded by scrolls or checkering. This small, simple pattern would make an excellent stock detail.

Checkering designs like this fish scale pattern can be used to decorate areas that might not accommodate other patterns.

Restoration Guns

Restoring an antique gun has more considerations that just deciding which pattern to use. You'll need to evaluate the gun's hardware and its existing stock. Any carving you do needs to match not only the gun's use but also the era in which it was originally used. Do your research.

Getting Started

As interest in gunstock carving grows, so do the options available to carvers as they decide where to start the process. Today, carvers can choose to start from blanks, from precarved blanks, or from kits. As before, knowing your skill level will help you decide.

Blanks are simply pieces of wood that have been cut to the correct length and width and may or may not have a general outline drawn on the surface. If you choose to start from a blank, you will need access to a band saw so you can rough cut the shape of the gunstock and some general carving tools to remove the excess wood and sand the gunstock smooth. Blanks are ideal for advanced and expert carvers who are working with highly figured wood, because they can then determine which part of the wood will best show off the grain.

Precarved, or preshaped, blanks have been cut, carved to shape, and sanded. When they arrive from the vendor, precarved blanks will need some additional cuts made with woodworking tools to fit the barrel and other hardware of the gun, and then some light sanding and a thorough wipe down with a tack cloth. This option is a time-saver for a busy woodcarver of any skill level. Some suppliers may make the cuts for you for an additional fee.

PHOTOS COURTESY OF CECIL FREDI

Gunstocks carved by Cecil Fredi go through a long process: from stump (top), to drying wood (middle), to stock (bottom).

When you order stock blanks or preshaped blanks, be aware that they are sized for special rifle manufactures, types, and series; be sure to order a stock made for your specific rifle.

Kits include a precarved blank and all the hardware to go with it, plus the predrilled holes and precut grooves. The barrel may or may not be included. Read the supplier's description carefully. Woodcarvers can focus almost entirely on the carving process with this option.

While you may be tempted to save the cost of materials and pick up your grandfather's shotgun as one of your first carving projects, don't do it. Old guns may be considered antiques and are often very valuable.

PHOTO COURTESY OF WHITE CREEK GUNSTOCK BLANKS

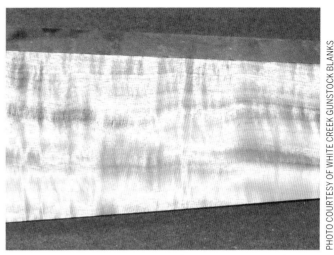

A windowpane myrtle wood blank is ready to be marked up for band sawing.

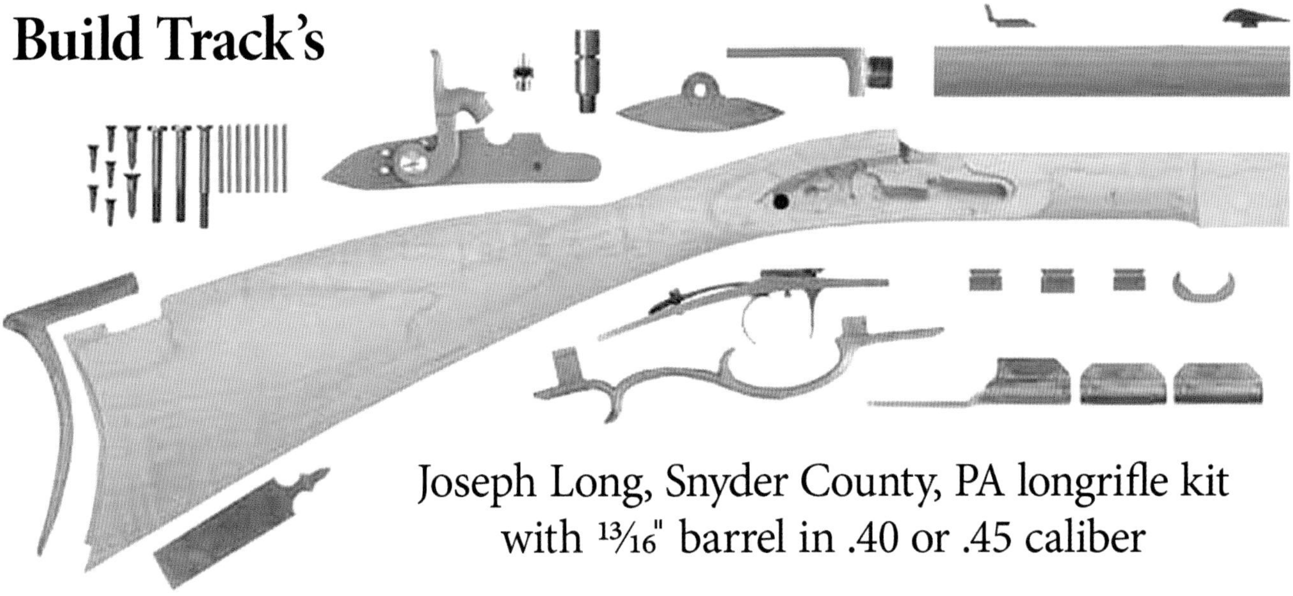

Build Track's
Joseph Long, Snyder County, PA longrifle kit
with 13/16" barrel in .40 or .45 caliber

PHOTO COURTESY OF TRACK OF THE WOLF

Gun kits, complete with the preshaped gunstock and all the hardware, are available through specialty retailers.

Wood Choices

The ideal woods for gunstock carving are hardwoods that will hold detail well. Walnut, cherry, maple, and myrtle are all good choices. If you are a beginning woodcarver, you will want to choose one of the softer hardwoods, maple for example, to ensure a successful project.

Walnut is perhaps the most esteemed wood for gunstock carving, and because of its dense grain, is also the hardest wood to carve. Many species are available, including black walnut, English walnut, Circassian walnut, Turkish walnut, and Bastogne walnut.

Maple and cherry hardwoods are readily available. Maple species to consider, mostly light in color and some with highly figured variations, include Western broad-leaf, red, sugar, and curly. Cherry, especially wild black cherry, can provide a deep red color. Other species to look for include black cherry and western Pennsylvania cherry.

White ash, a strong and resilient wood, is another good choice for gunstock carving. Its light color can showcase the beautiful natural color variations in the wood and serve as a good backdrop for an intricate carving.

Myrtle is less popular for gunstock carving, but is a beautiful hardwood. It has a light background with black, red, or brown variations. Tiger myrtle, from long-growing trees, is a very expensive species to carve.

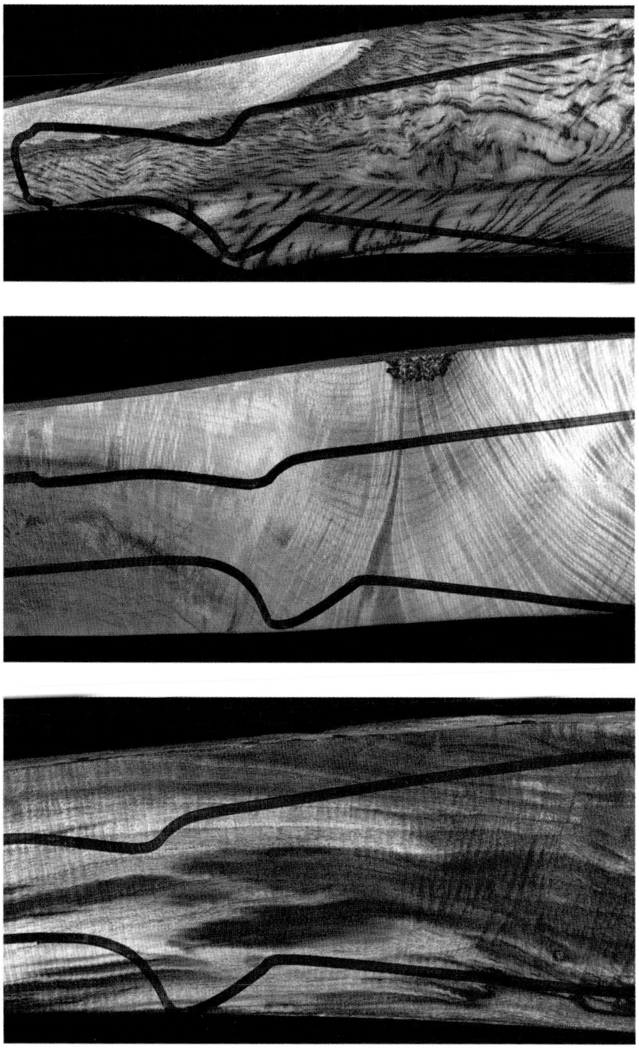

PHOTOS COURTESY OF CECIL FREDI.

A gunstock blank pattern placed on three different species of myrtle shows how varied wood can be. Top to bottom: tiger myrtle, dark myrtle, and myrtle (grain affected by a knot).

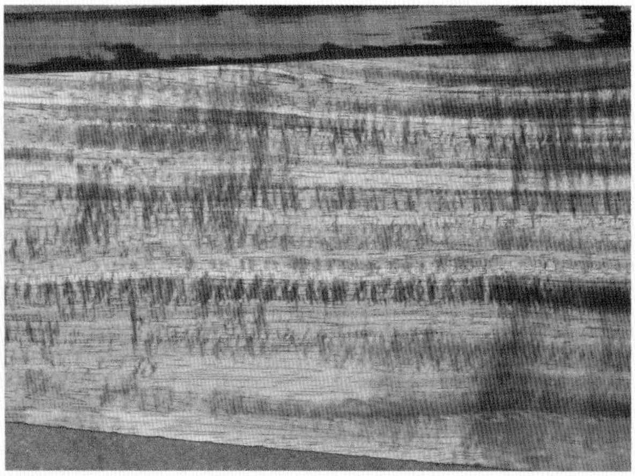

PHOTO COURTESY OF WHITE CREEK GUNSTOCK BLANKS

Rare Woods

Some species of wood are available in limited quantities due to timbering restrictions and diseases that have decimated forests. The cutting of Hawaiian koa trees, which grow only on the Hawaiian Islands, is now illegal; only certified dead trees can be harvested and very few trees reach the maturity necessary for larger projects. This koa blank has been air drying since 1978. The wood is very dense and carves well, but the natural silica embedded in the wood from the volcanic soil in which the tree grows can dull tools quickly.

Figure and grading

Natural color variations in wood are referred to as "figure." Woods with lots of variation are called "highly figured." While highly figured wood is very attractive, it may not be the best choice for highly detailed patterns because the elements of a design can become lost in the variations of the wood. Choose highly figured wood for simpler patterns; less figured wood is ideal for intricate patterns with a lot of detail.

Figure also determines the grade of the wood you are purchasing. Most grading systems follow a numbered scale, with 1 being the fanciest, or most highly figured, wood. Some grading systems will use letters, with AAA being the top, or exhibitionist, grade. Read about the scale on the suppliers' websites to determine how their wood is graded. Generally speaking, the more figured the wood is, the more expensive it will be.

Some vendors use separate grading systems for plain wood. Instead of letters or numbers, simple identifying phrases describe the quality of the wood. The lowest grade of plain wood, sometimes referred to as "low utility grade" or "utility grade," commonly reveals severe defects or serious blemishes. The blank may also have been glued together or otherwise repaired. These woods may not be ideal for a finished project, but they make excellent practice pieces for beginning woodcarvers. The top two grades will generally be blemish free, with the highest grade possibly having some light figuring or mineral streaking.

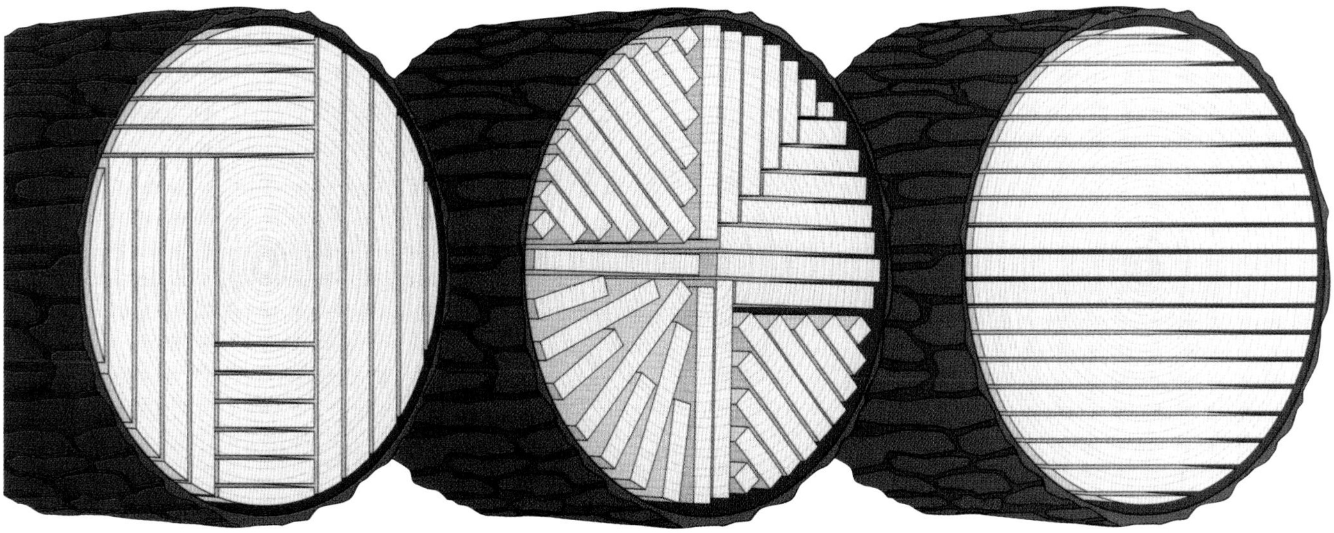

How a tree is cut plays a big part in the appearance of stock wood. This diagram shows three different saw cuts through a log. Because wood is a natural product, predicting exactly what a blank will look like is impossible, but stockmakers can give you a good idea of how nice a blank will be by looking at the grains and the amount of dark streaking.

Practice First

Every carver can benefit from a trial run before putting tools to the wood of an actual gunstock. Choose a low grade, less expensive wood to work out the difficult areas of a pattern or to practice repetitive cuts. Consider a bit of practice before you begin as a time to warm up your carving skills and build your confidence.

Tool Choices

The patterns in this book were specifically designed to be relief carved with hand tools; however, they may also be used with power carving tools, woodburners, laser engravers, and sand blasters. Your choice of tools should be based upon a combination of your familiarity and skill level with a certain method and on the placement of the pattern on the firearm. A deeply carved relief scene is not ideal on the cheek rest of a gun, but it may be suitable on the grip. Woodburned or laser engraved details that are close to the surface are better choices for some areas, depending on the use of the gun.

Relief carving is done with knives and hand-held gouges that have a V-, U-, or flat-shaped edge. The cuts allow the image to stand above the background of the wood. In gunstock carving, a narrow area around the image is generally removed to give the effect of relief carving. Relief carvings can be carved quite deeply into the wood—as deep as ¼" (0.5cm) on gunstocks—giving the finished scene more depth. Outline patterns are ideal for relief carving. Beginners may wish to create a shaded drawing of the pattern as a gauge for depth.

Mini hand push tools are ideal for smaller projects.

PHOTO COURTESY OF WOODCARVERSSUPPLY.COM

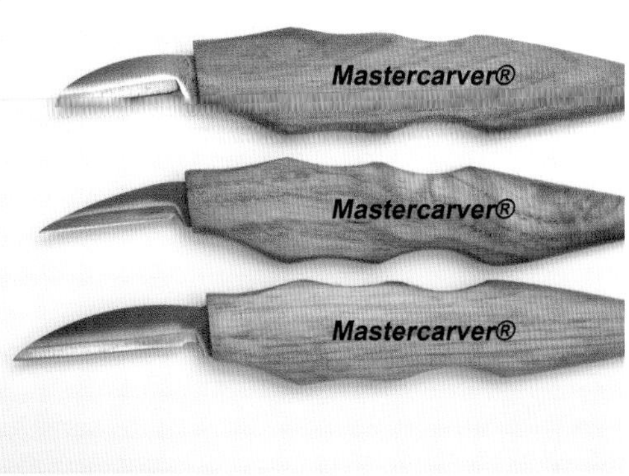

PHOTO COURTESY OF WOODCARVERSSUPPLY.COM

Good quality knives with comfortable grips are essential for hand carved projects.

PHOTO COURTESY OF WOODCARVERSSUPPLY.COM

An ideal set of tools for relief carving includes a variety of gouges. This 10-piece set includes a chisel, a V-tool, and a handful of U-shaped gouges.

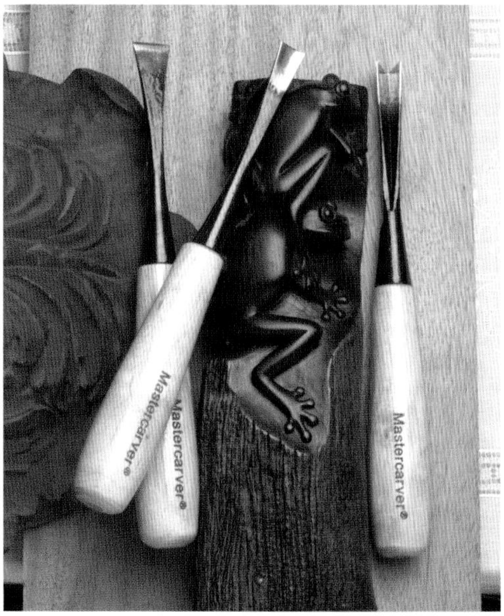

PHOTO COURTESY OF WOODCARVERSSUPPLY.COM

Buy the best tools you can afford within your budget, even if it means buying only one or two tools at a time.

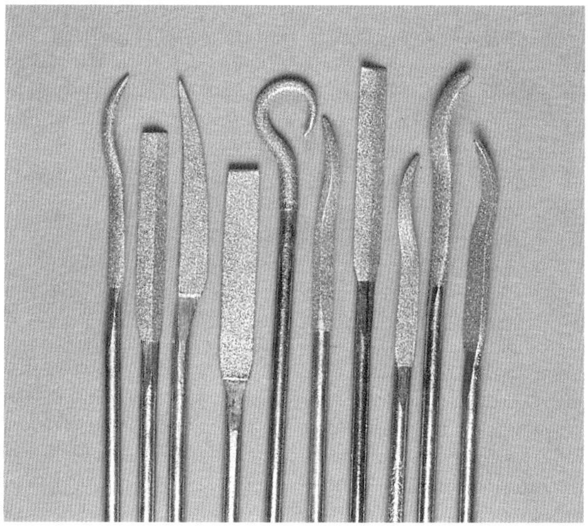

PHOTO COURTESY OF *WOODCARVERSSUPPLY.COM*

Files are available in fine grit, like this 10-piece set, and coarse grit and are handy for removing wood in small areas of relief carving.

PHOTO COURTESY OF *WOODCARVERSSUPPLY.COM*

This 8-tool detail set includes some of the most useful tools from 1/16" to 3/8" (2 to 10mm) wide.

Checkering is a series of lines, either parallel or worked in a crossing diamond pattern, that create a texture for a stronger hand grip on the rifle. It is worked with a special set of tools called checkering gouges. These gouges have an arm that drops into the last checkering line to ensure accurate placement of the next line you cut. The checkering tool is a fine V-tool that leaves a clean V-shaped cut.

You can also add texture to the hand grip using a fish scale pattern, a small carving with a round gouge–cut background, or by creating a small pebble texture.

Power carving can make fast work of a pattern and give your end product a smoother finish. Again, your choice of tools should be based on the use of the gun and the effect you are trying to create. Some power carvers, like Bill Janney from Arizona, use dental power tools to remove wood. He finds that the speed and accuracy of the tools are essential in creating fine details. This method of carving can also provide the deep relief that can be achieved with hand carving tools.

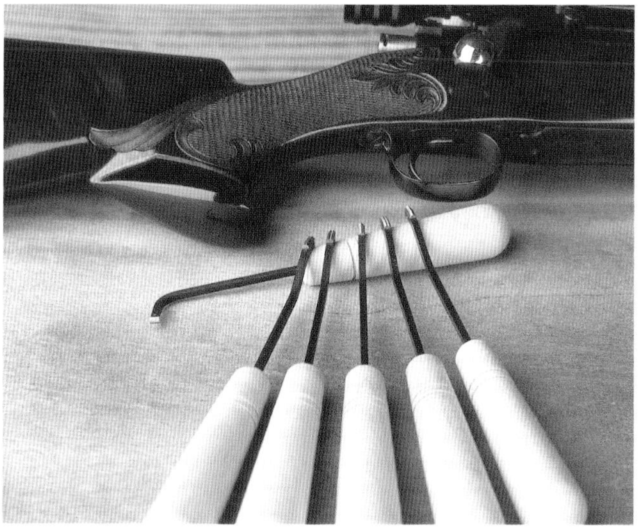

PHOTO COURTESY OF *WOODCARVERSSUPPLY.COM*

Checkering tools can be used to create a repeating grid pattern on a gunstock. Some carvers find that file-like checkering tools are an excellent choice for the fine detailed carving of fur, hair, and feathers.

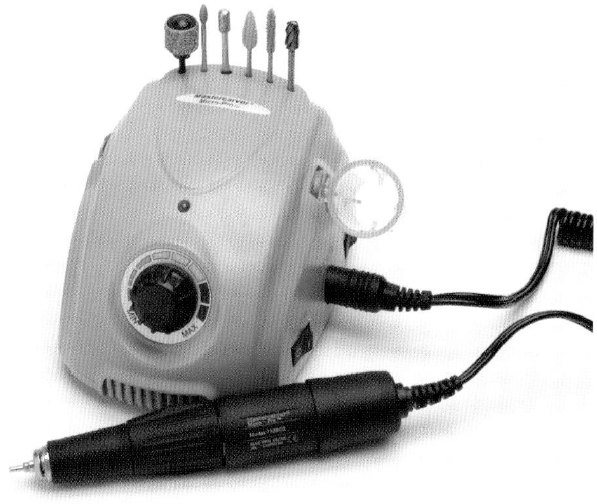

PHOTO COURTESY OF *WOODCARVERSSUPPLY.COM*

Power carving tools have a number of bits that speed up the removal of wood and creation of fine textures.

Rather than carving into the wood for a relief effect, a sepia-toned shaded drawing can be created on the surface of the wood using woodburning tools.

PHOTO COURTESY OF WEST VIRGINIA WOOD ARTS

Patterns can be taken to a laser engraver for a delicate, low relief reproduction of personalized artwork. This image was created from a photograph, but any shaded pattern will also work well.

Woodburning does not provide a deep relief effect. Instead it creates a sepia-toned shaded drawing on the surface of the wood, similar to an etching. Most of the wood removal is done very close to the surface of the wood. Hotter tips and more pressure create a darker and slightly deeper cut. Carvers who would like to use these patterns for woodburning may find it useful to shade the patterns as a guide for hotter and cooler burns. Woodburning can be done with a unit that provides power and a hand-held tool that makes the burns. Various tips in different widths and shapes are available.

Laser engraving is similar in principle to woodburning, but its application is very different. Laser engraving creates an extremely shallow carved image. In fact, according to Garry McKinney at West Virginia Wood Arts, most laser engraving is 40/1000" to 100/1000" deep; a laser engraving with a depth of 1/16" is considered very deep. The cost of a laser engraving machine—from $7,000 to $50,000—can be prohibitive for individual woodcarvers; however, some companies that cater to artists will make single items from a pattern upon request. Patterns must be converted to vector art (shading); the darker lines on a pattern instruct the engraving machine to make deeper cuts.

Sandblasting, where the design is masked off and wood around it is removed with a sand blaster, is another way to use these patterns on gunstocks. Again, the cost of the machinery is out of reach for most carvers, but like laser engraving companies, some sandblasting outfits will cater to individual artists.

Finishing

The best finishing method for gunstocks is a simple hand-rubbed wax or oil finish that will enhance the grain of the wood. Test the finish of your choice on scrap wood and conduct an Internet search or talk to the manufacturer about how a particular wax or oil holds up over time. Before you apply the finish according to the manufacturer's directions, lightly sand the wood, and then remove any wood dust with a tack cloth. Do not allow excess wax or oil to collect in the low spots of your carved design. Colored finishes, high-gloss finishes, and paints are to be avoided.

PART 2

Gunstock Carving Patterns

The patterns that follow feature traditional sportsman and hunting-related themes and are drawn with rifle stocks and relief carving in mind. However, small changes will make these patterns just as applicable to knife handles, pistol grips, and duck calls and equally usable with various wood carving methods including power carving, woodburning, and laser engraving.

As with any patterns, these patterns can also be altered to fit your needs. After assessing your skill level, you can simplify the pattern of your choice by removing elements or make it more complex by refining elements.

Be sure to match the type of pattern to the sport in which the firearm will be used—hunting dogs on a rifle used for deer hunting is not the best choice—and then alter the pattern to fit the gunstock. Try adding oak leaves or checkering to patterns that need a few more elements to fit the space on the gunstock. Leaves and checkering is also an attractive stand-alone design.

Most importantly, be creative and take your time. You are creating one-of-a-kind, personalized artwork that will be cherished for years to come.

Animal Patterns

Mule deer

White-tailed deer

White-tailed deer

Mule deer

White-tailed deer

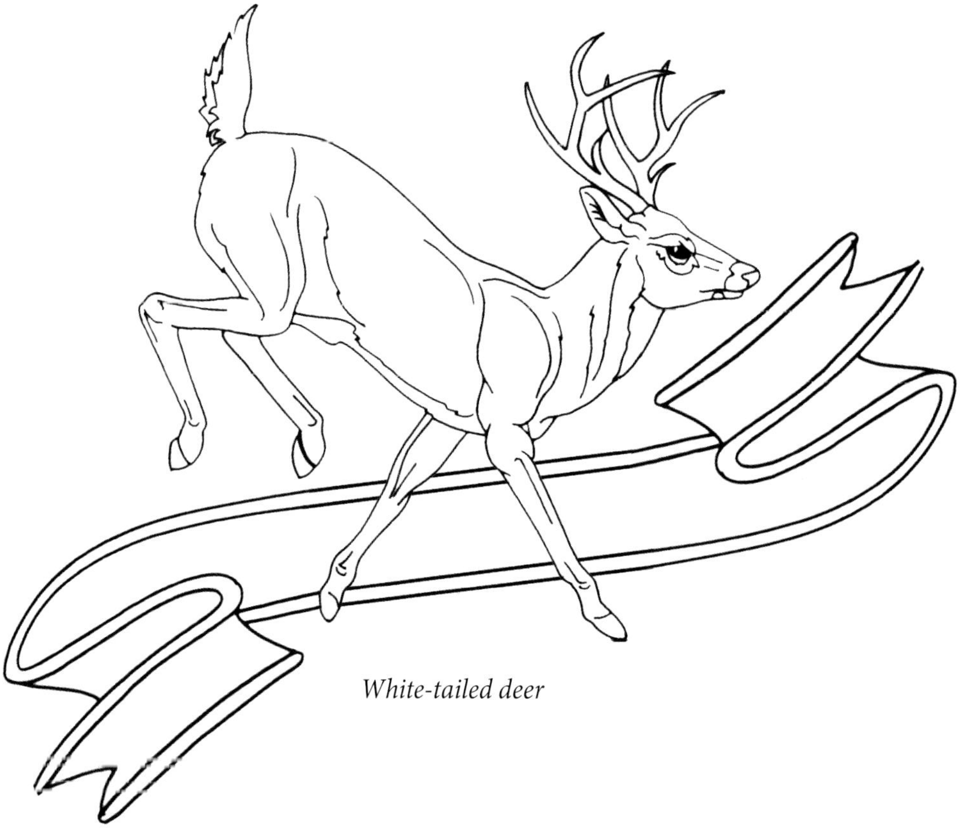

White-tailed deer

White-tailed deer

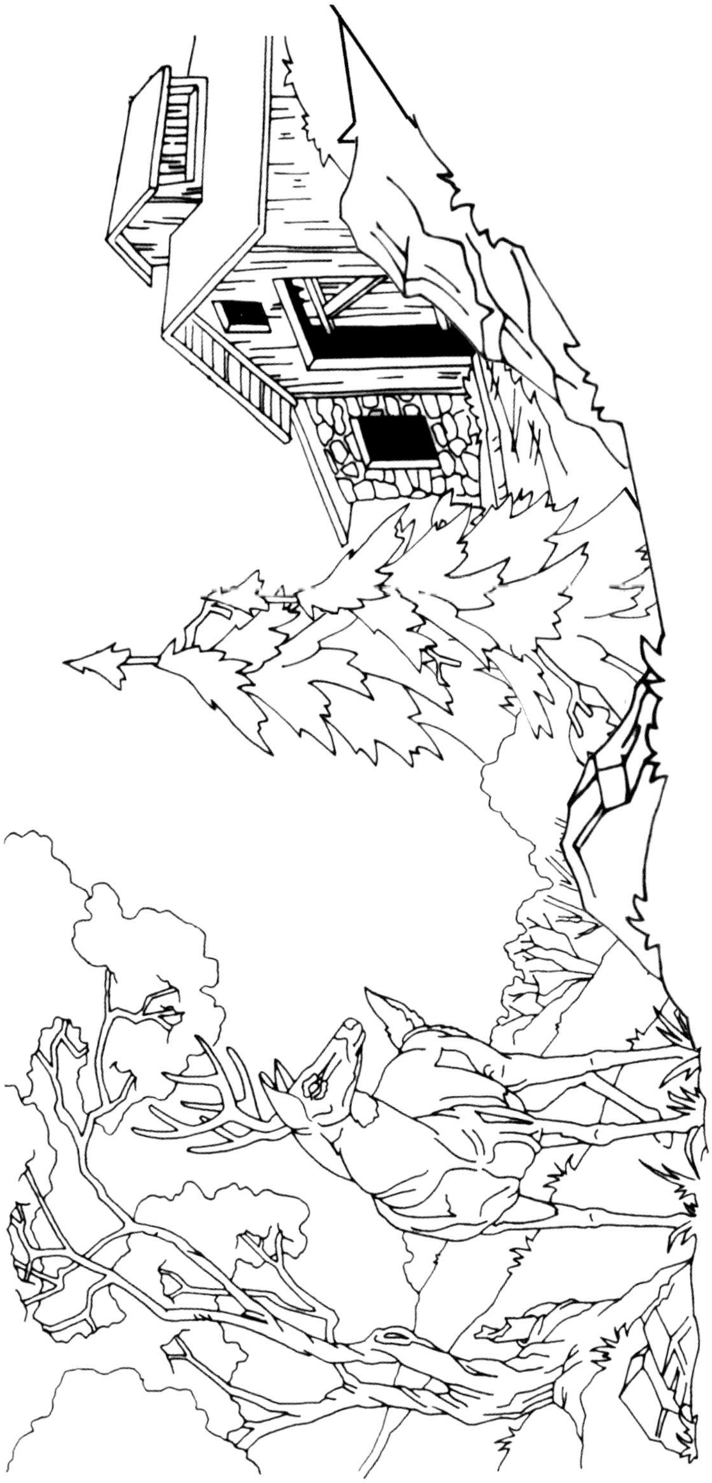

White-tailed deer

Elk

Elk

Buffalo

Moose

Puma and snake

Puma

Fighting bears

Mountain goats and puma

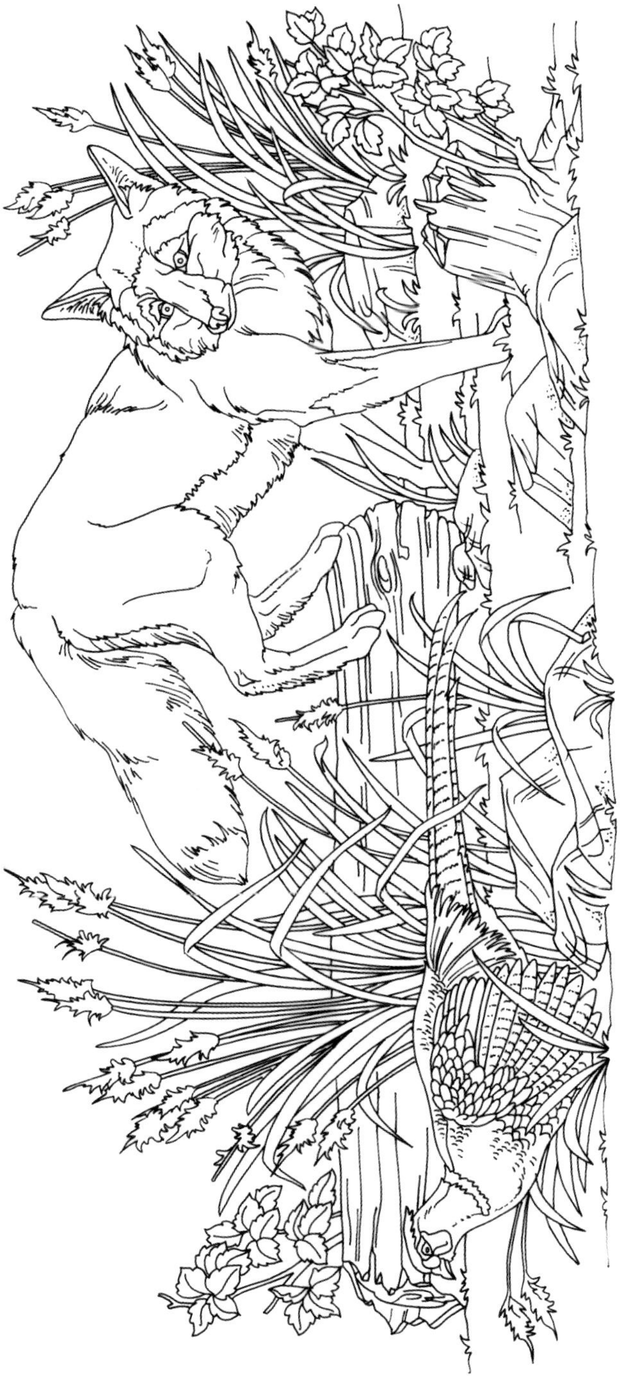

Fox and pheasant

Bobcat and pintail

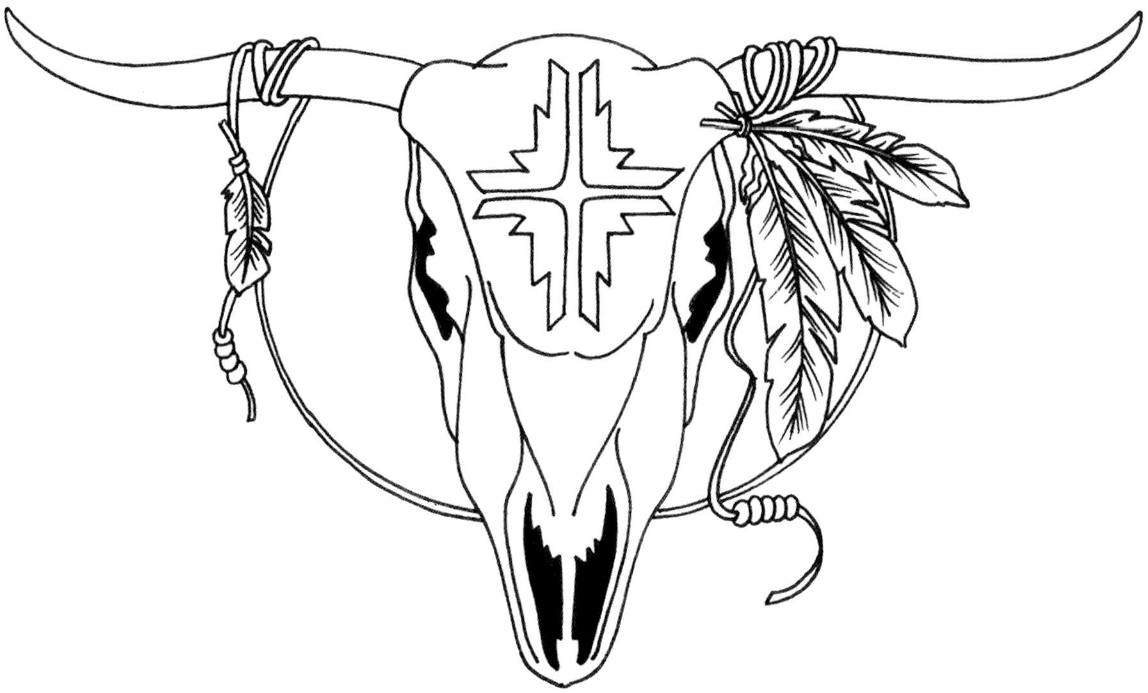

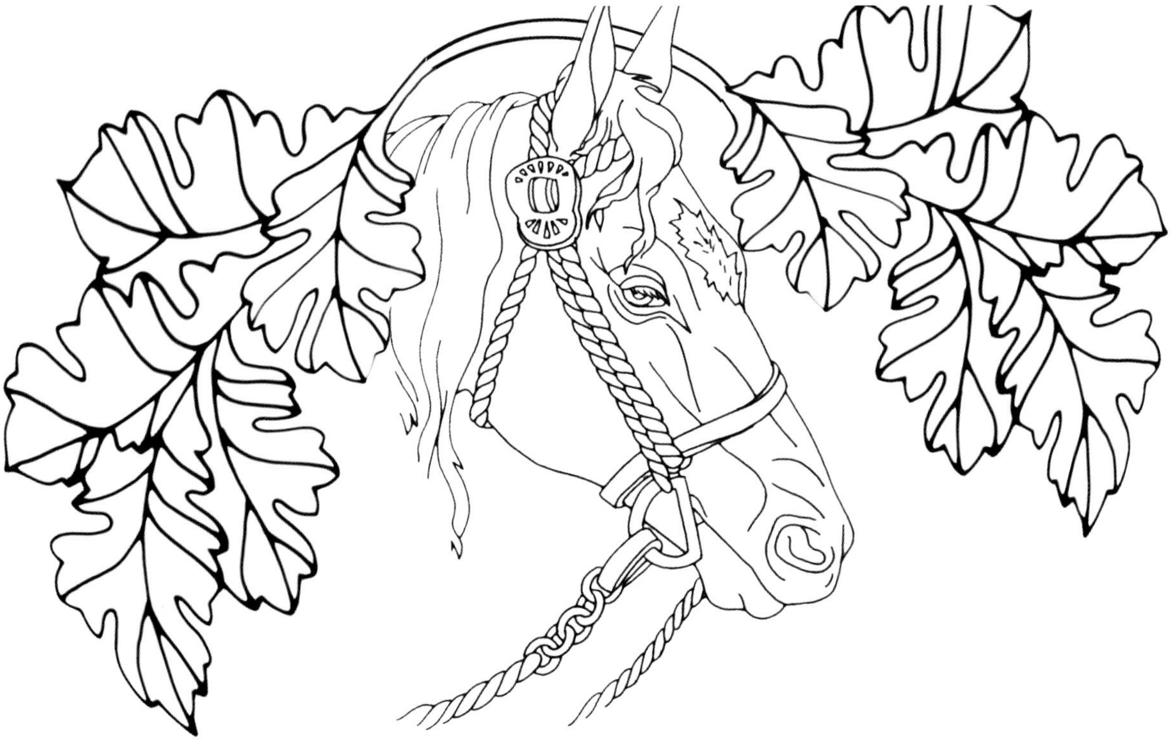

Bird and Waterfowl Patterns

Gun dog and quail

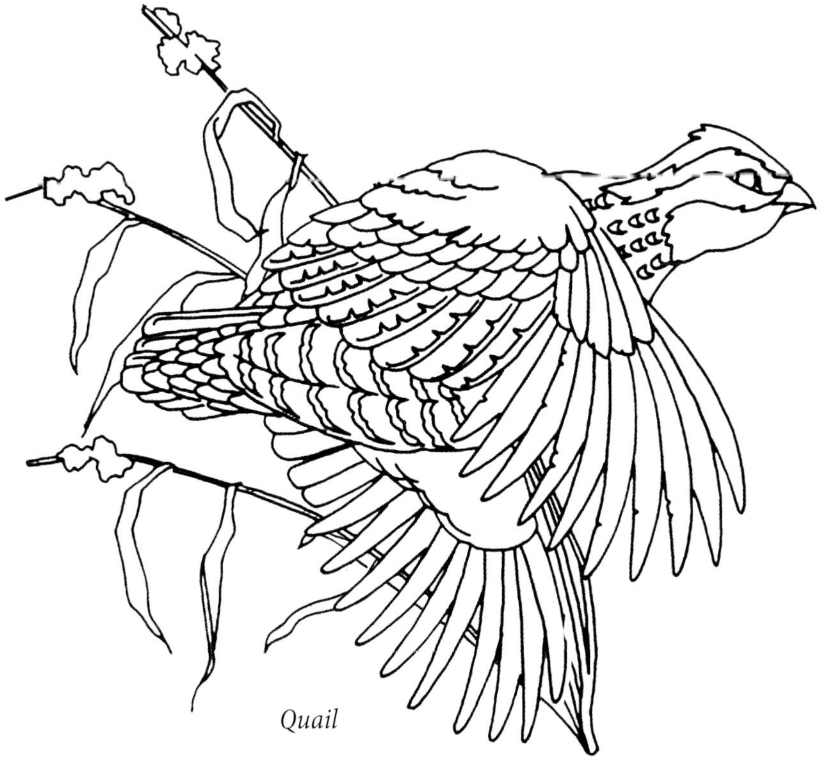

Quail

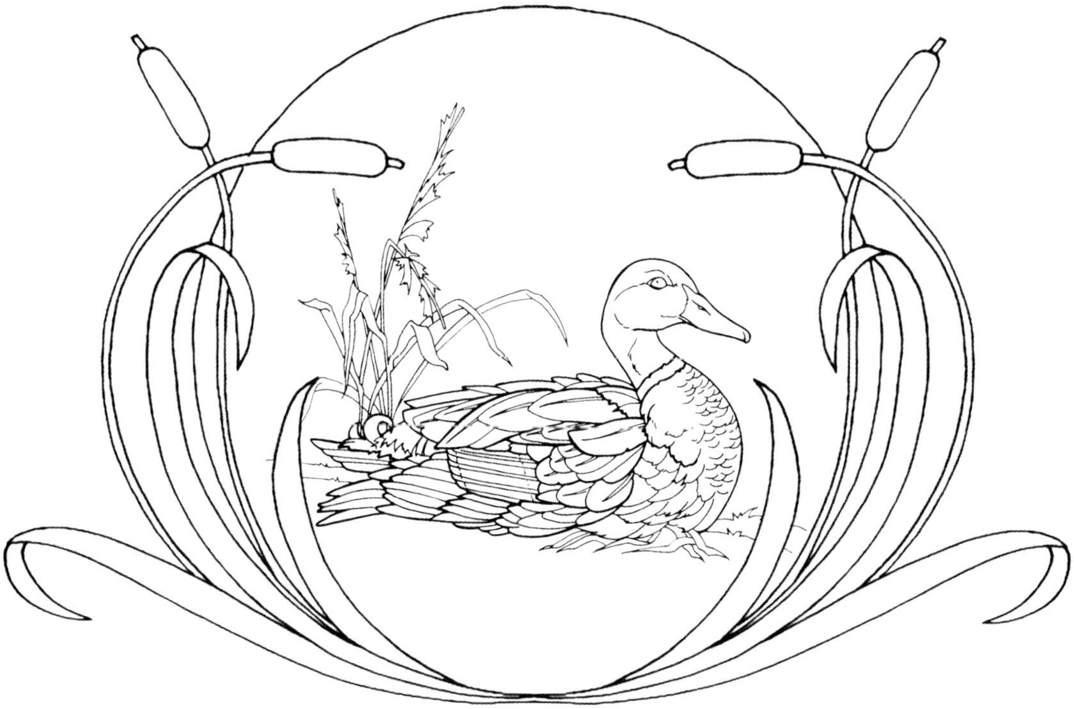

Mallard

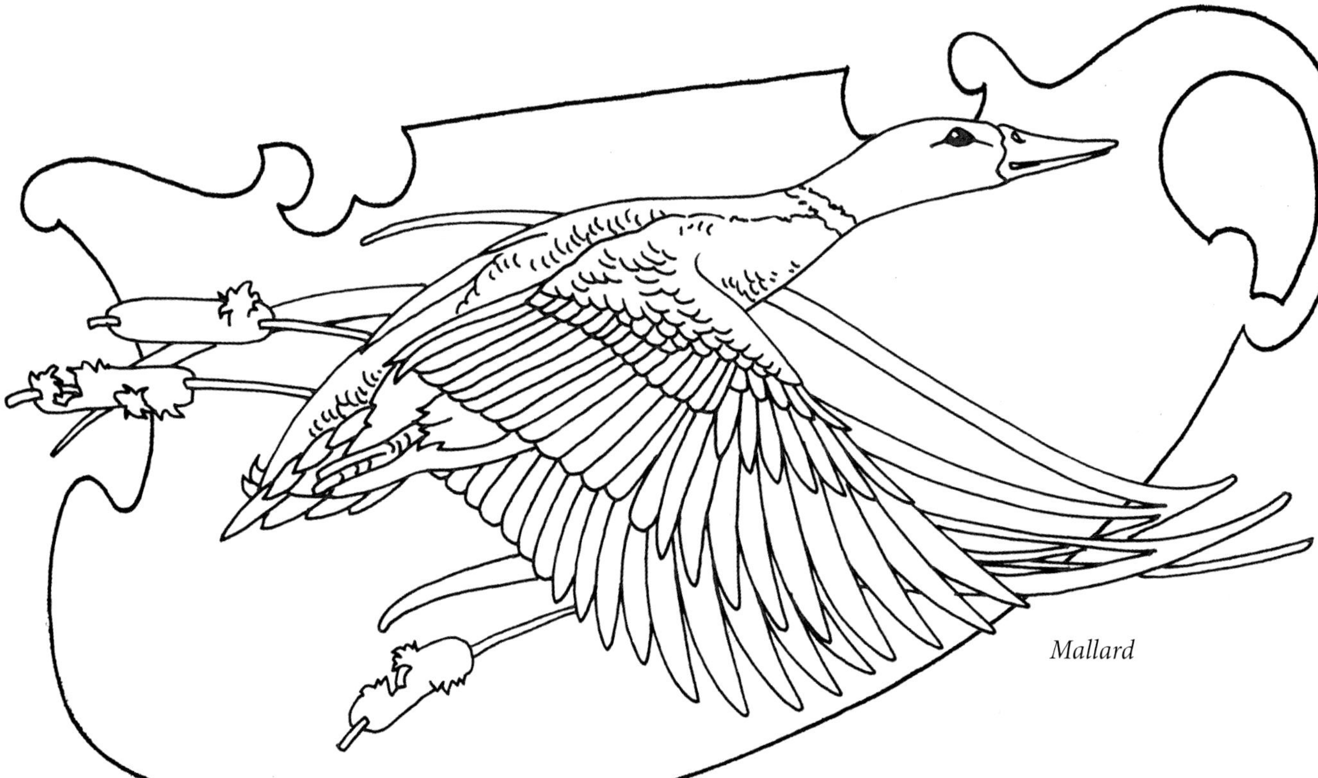

Mallard

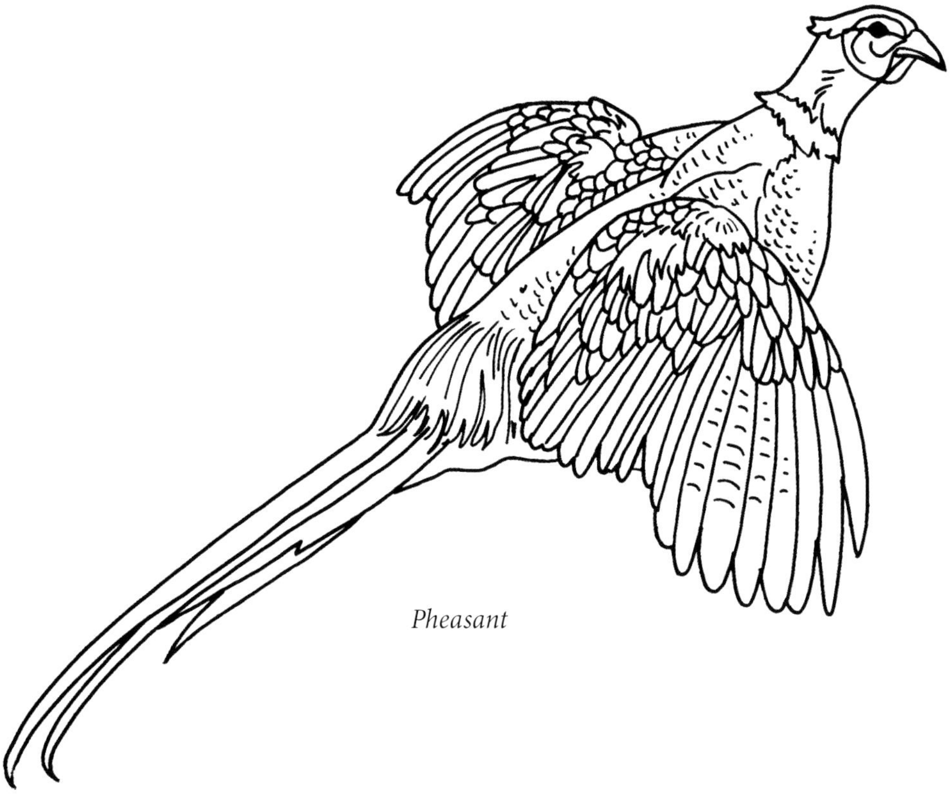

Pheasant

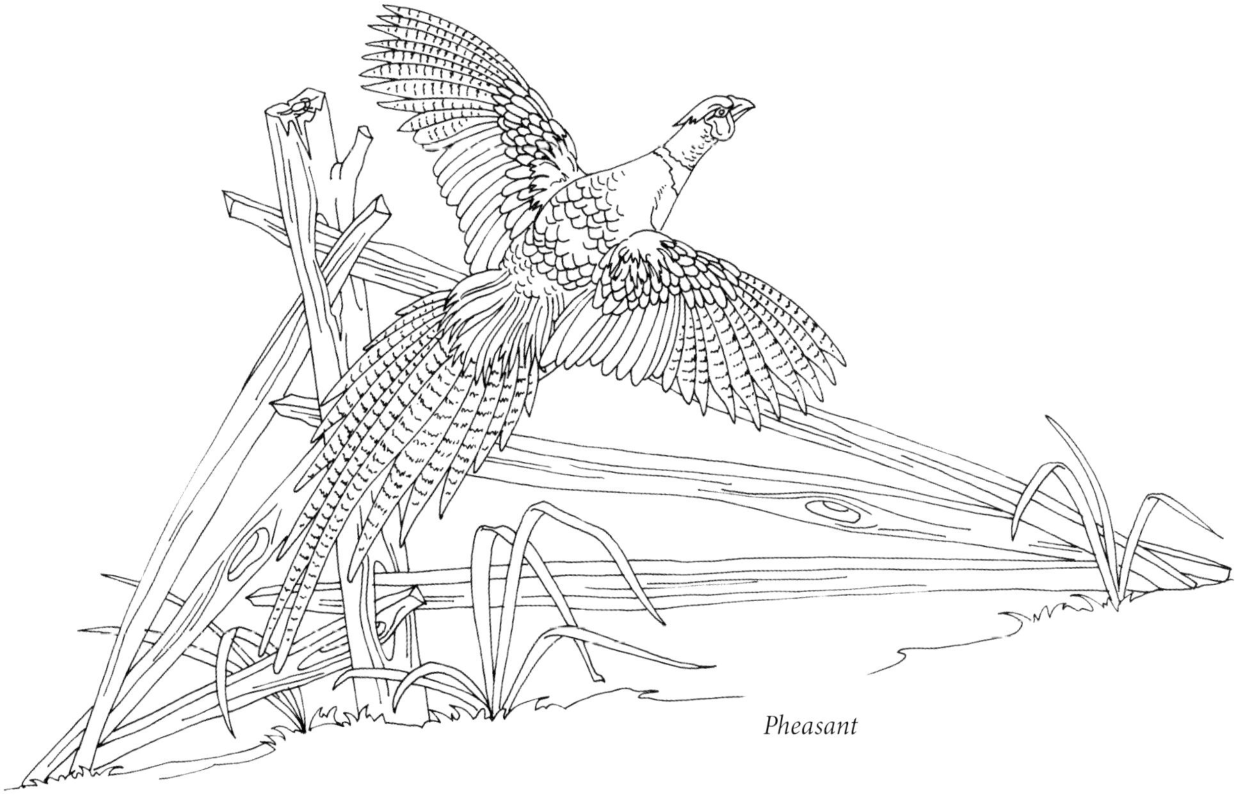

Pheasant

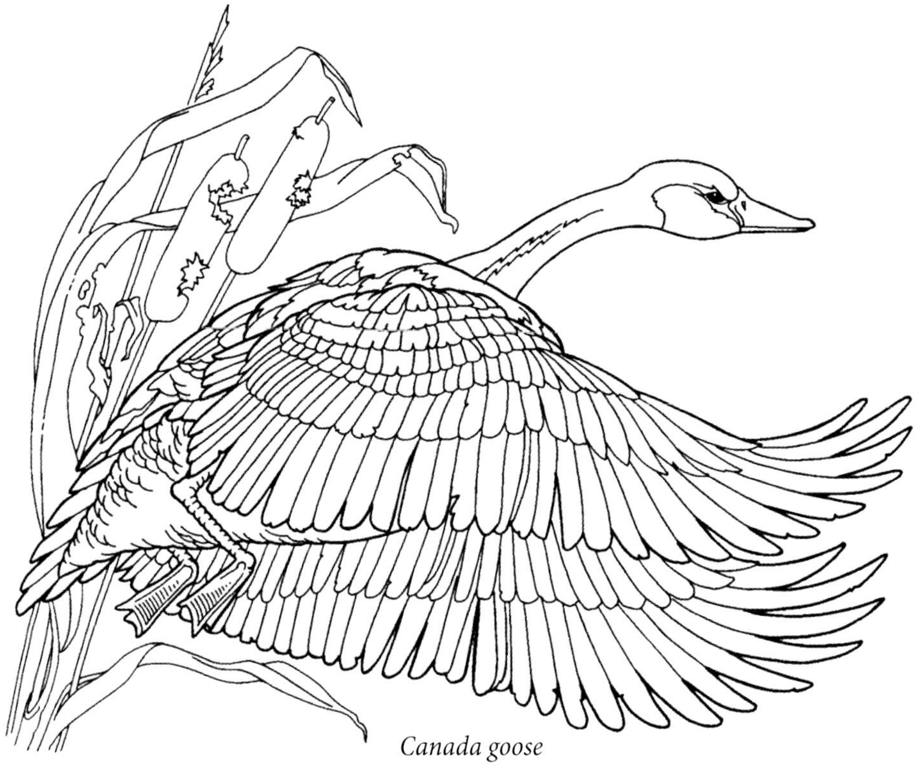

Canada goose

Mallard

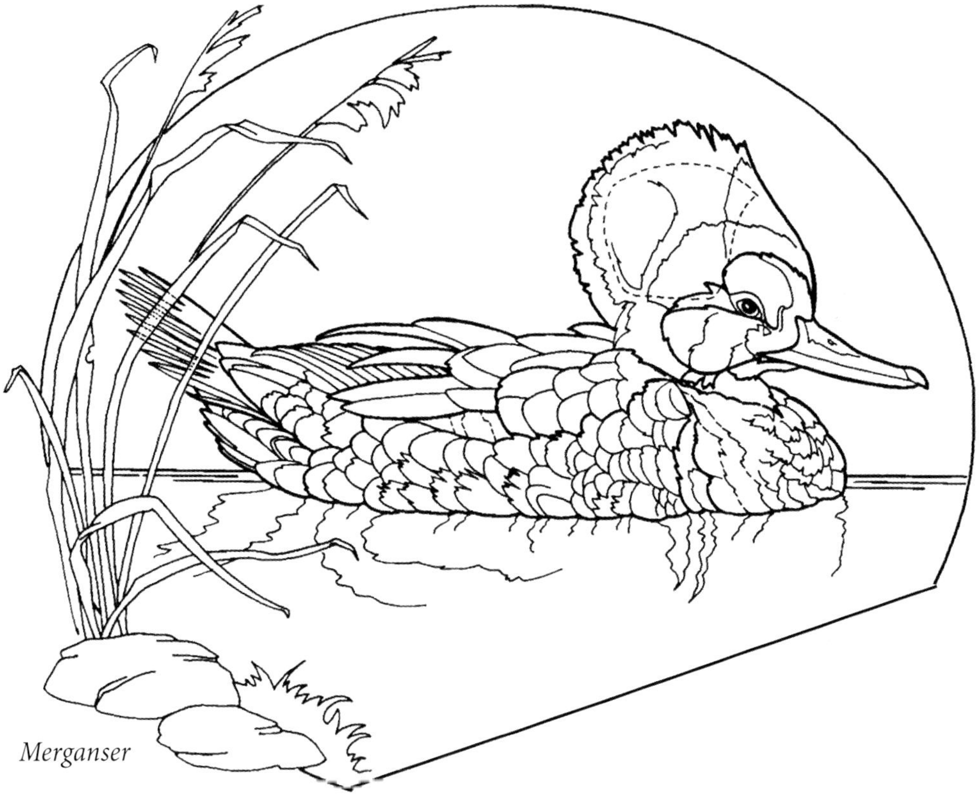

Merganser

Canvasback

Eagle and Scroll Patterns

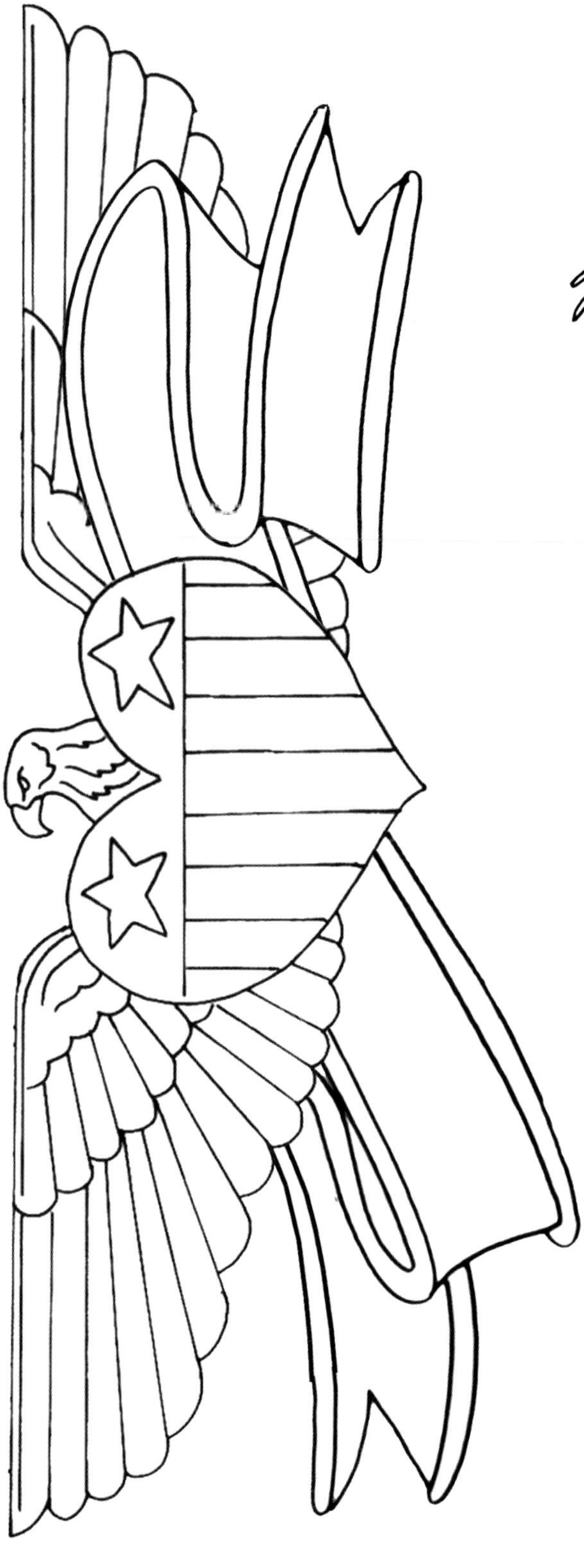

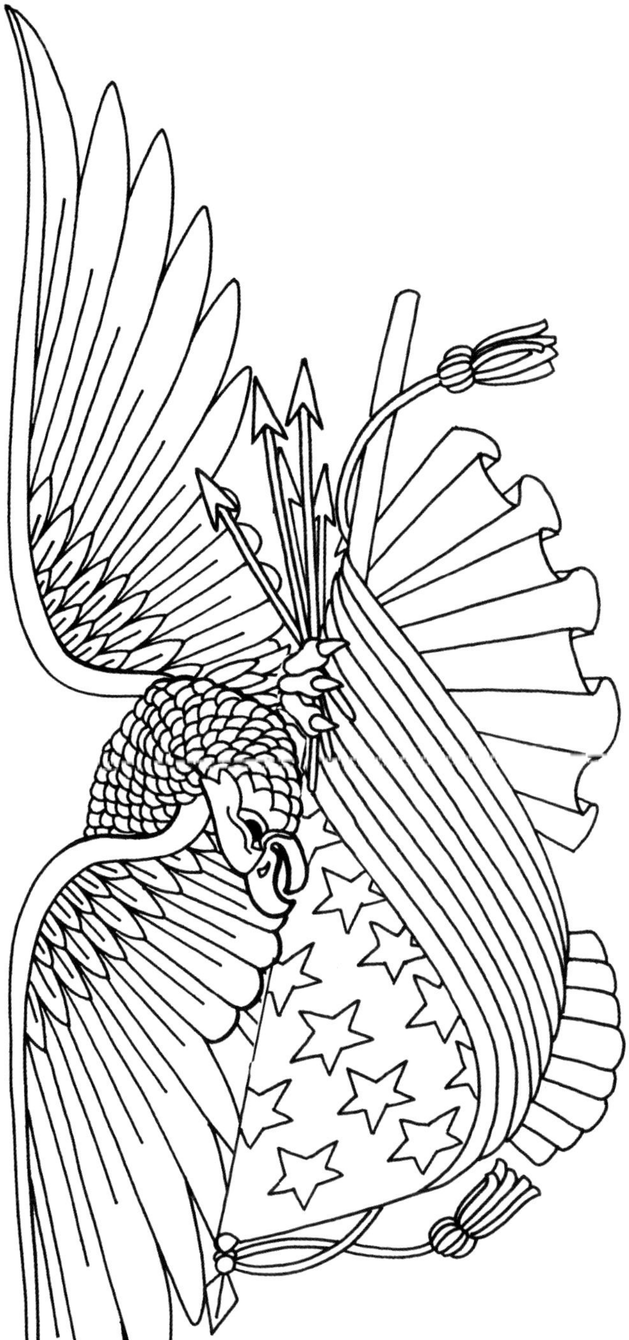

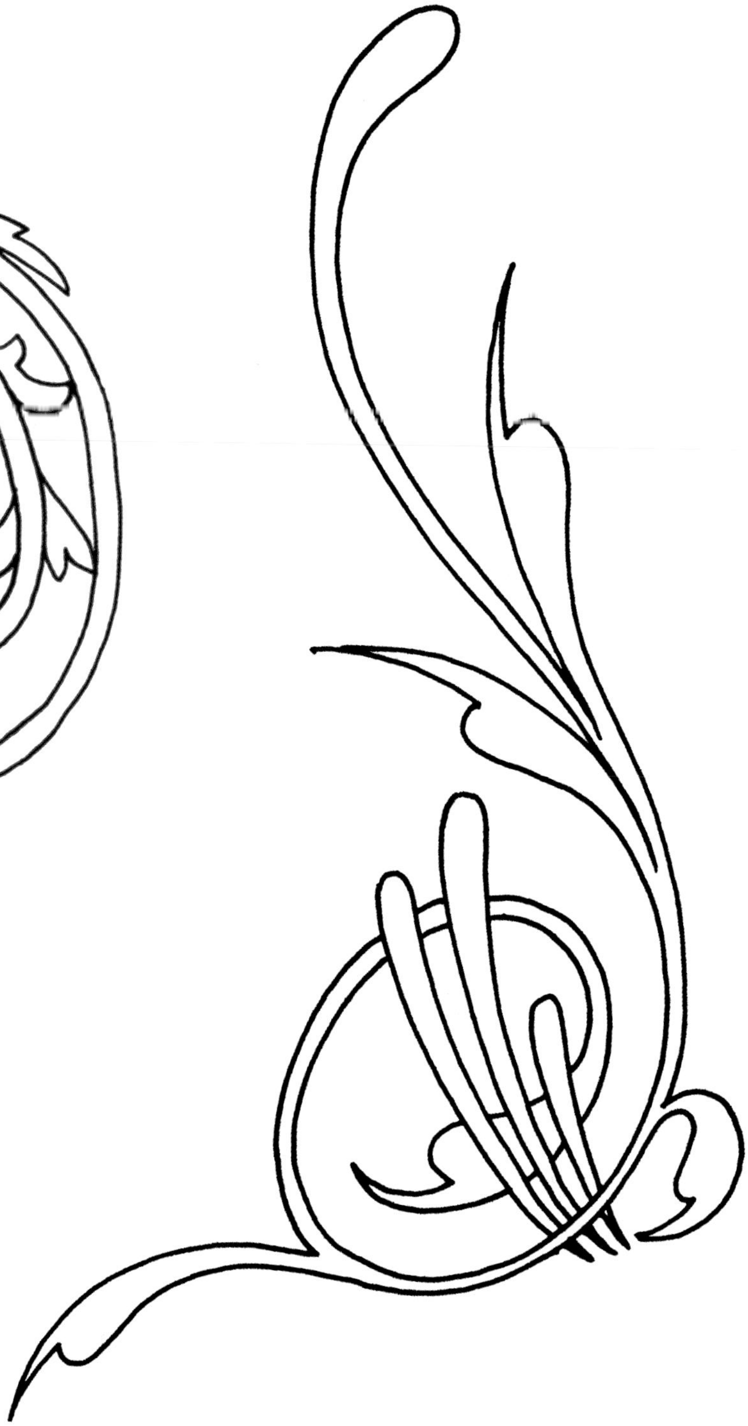

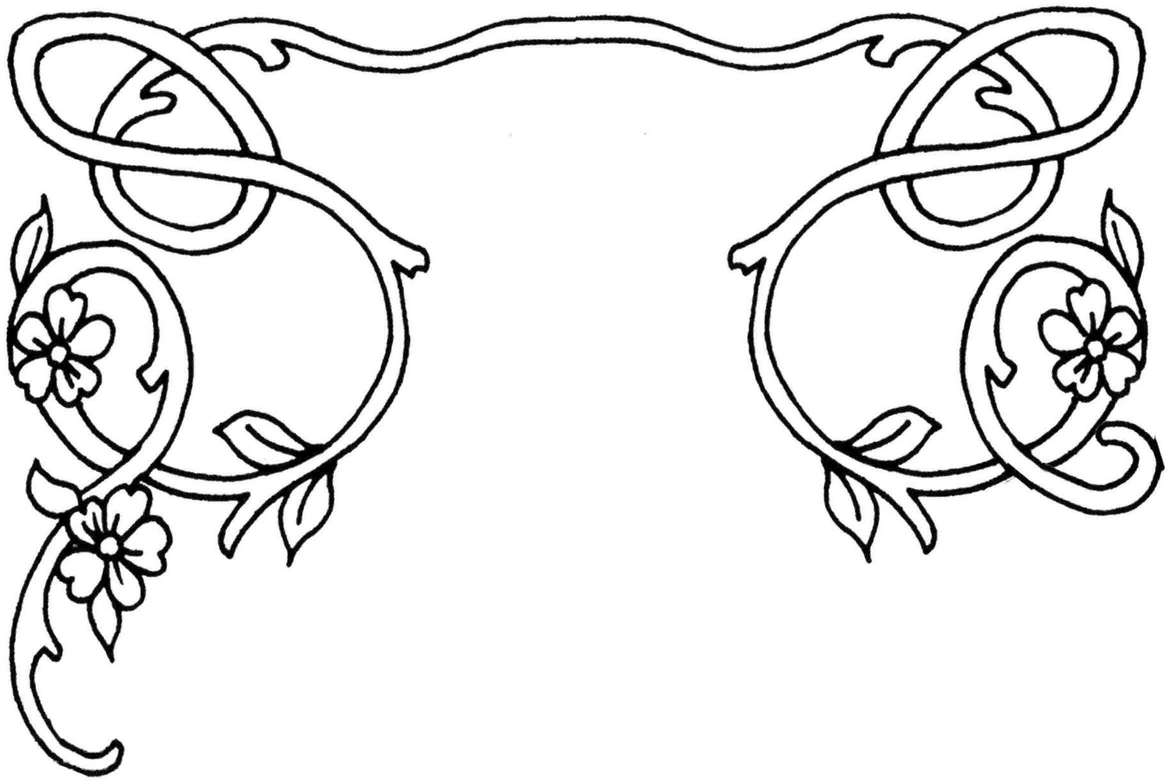

Butt End Patterns

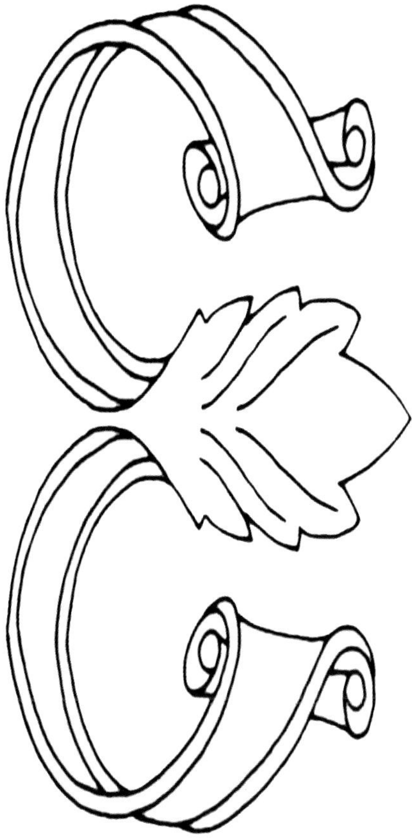

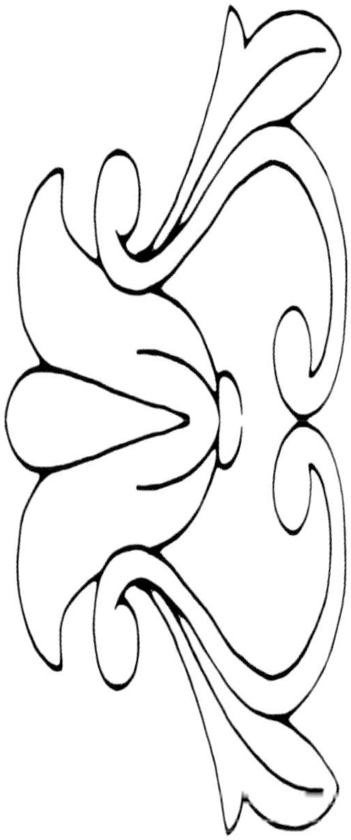

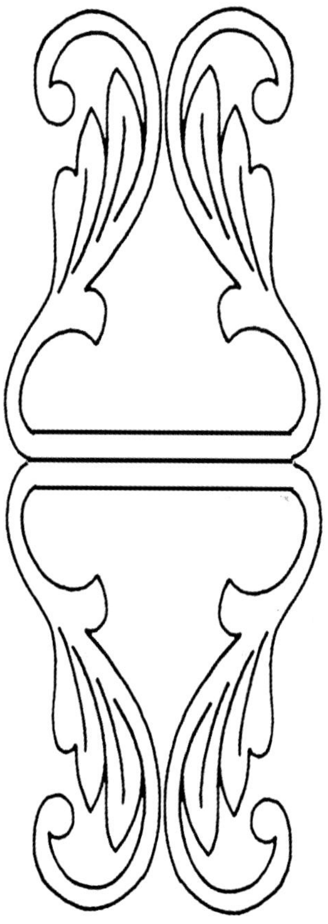

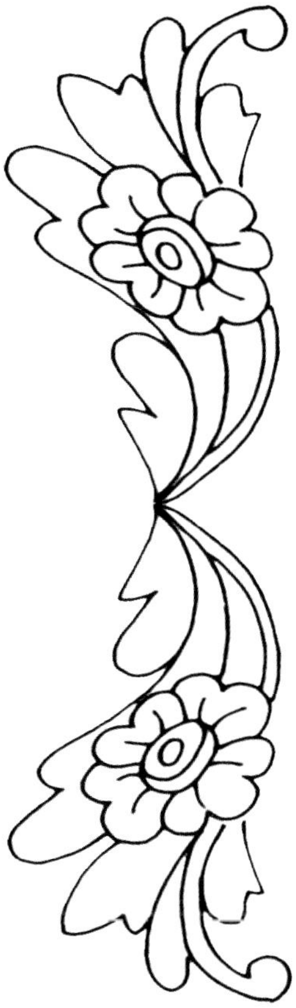

Panel Patterns

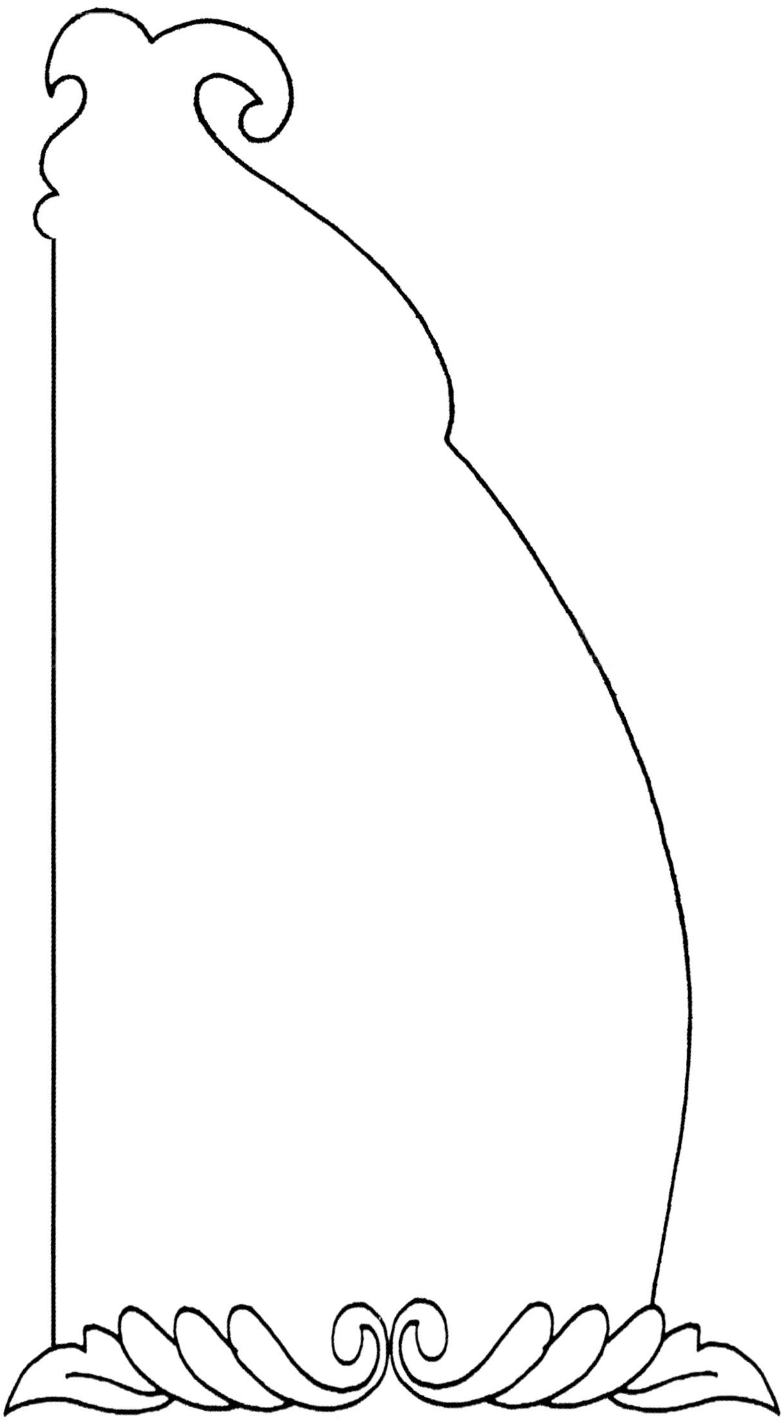

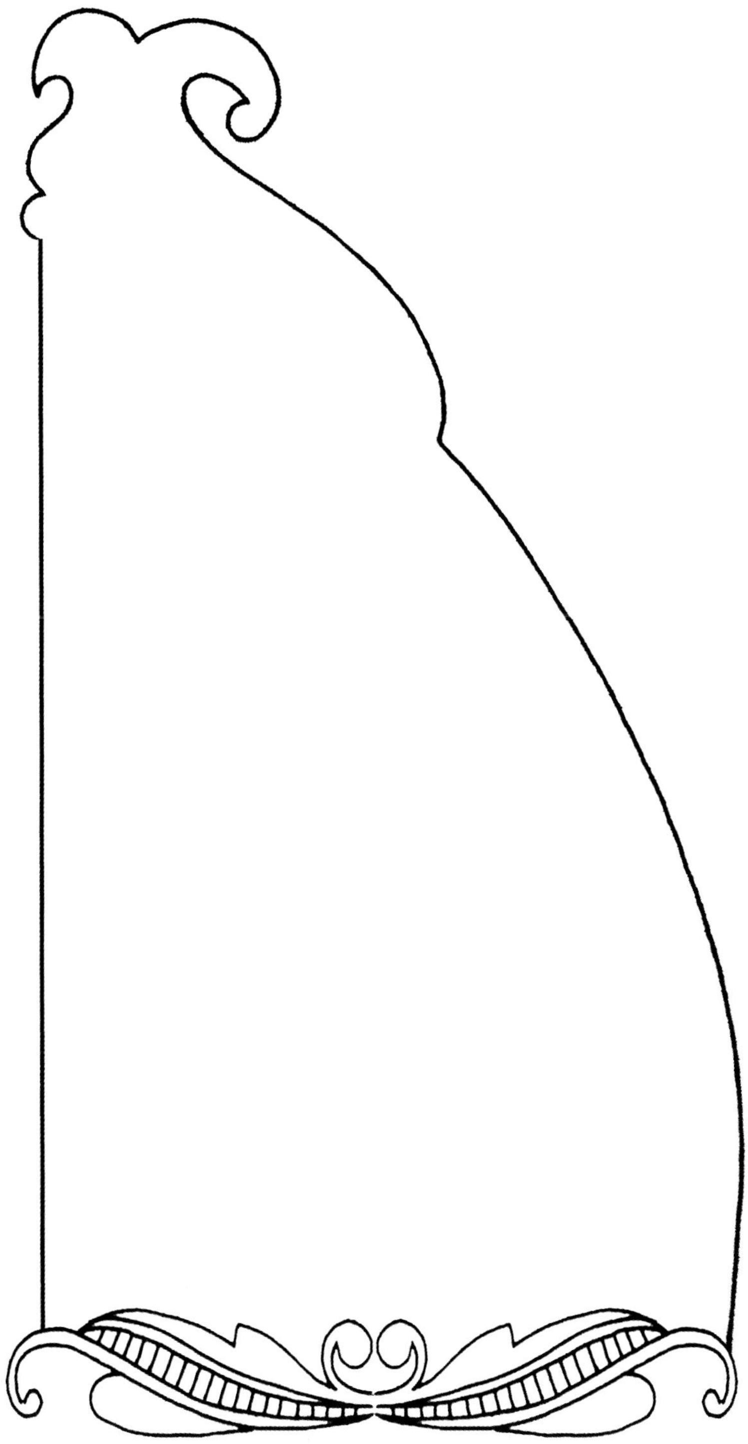

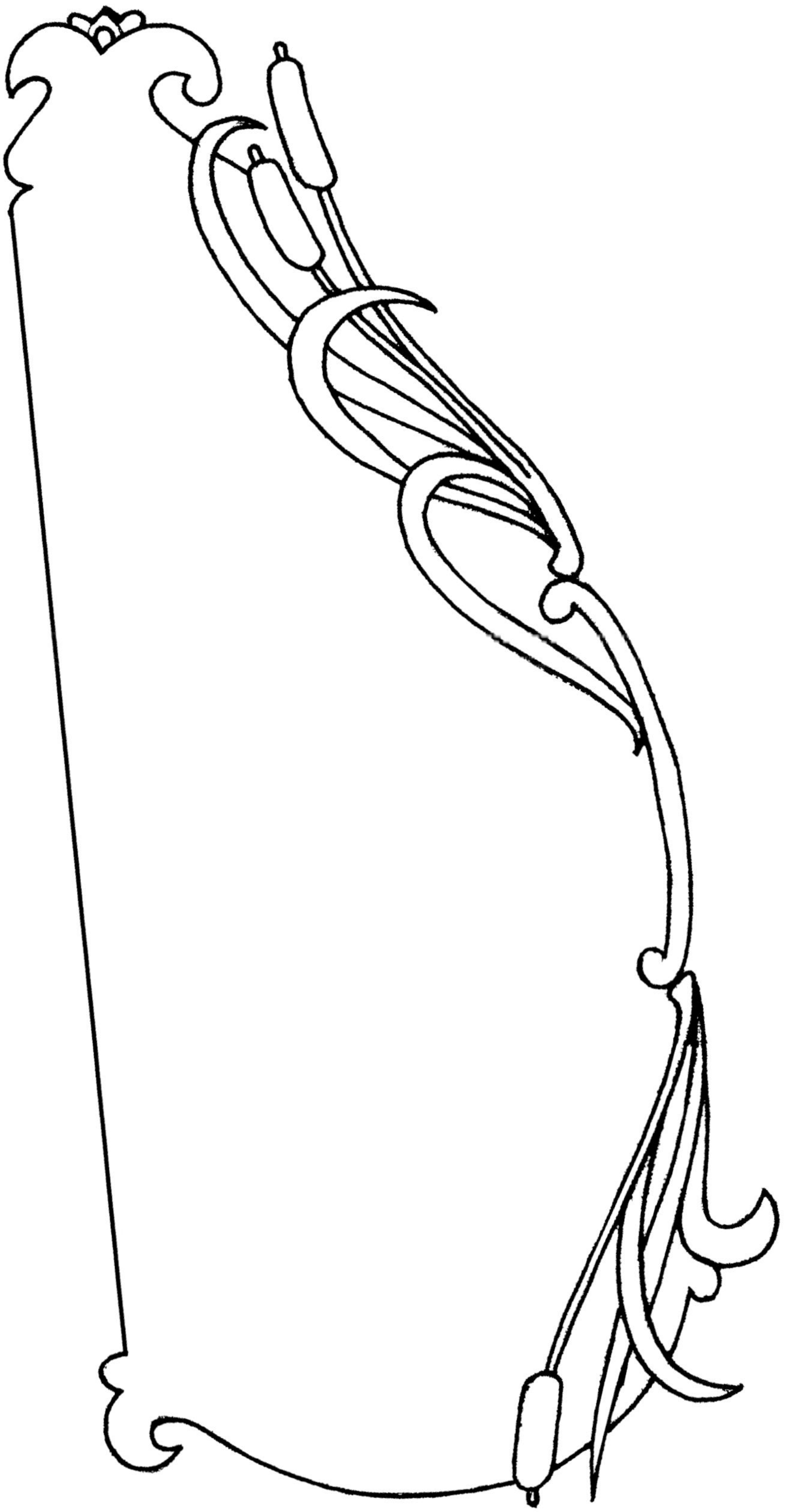

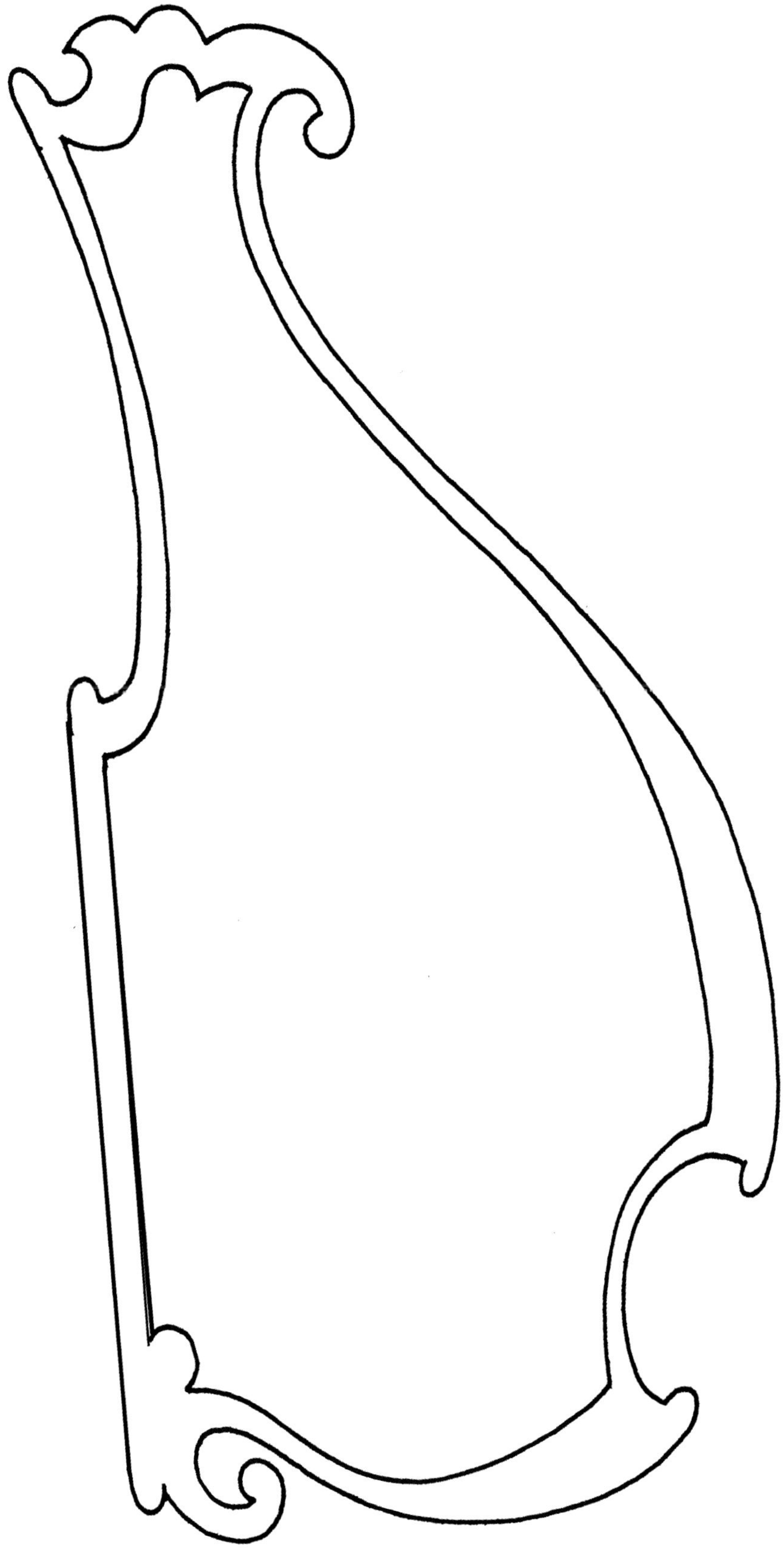

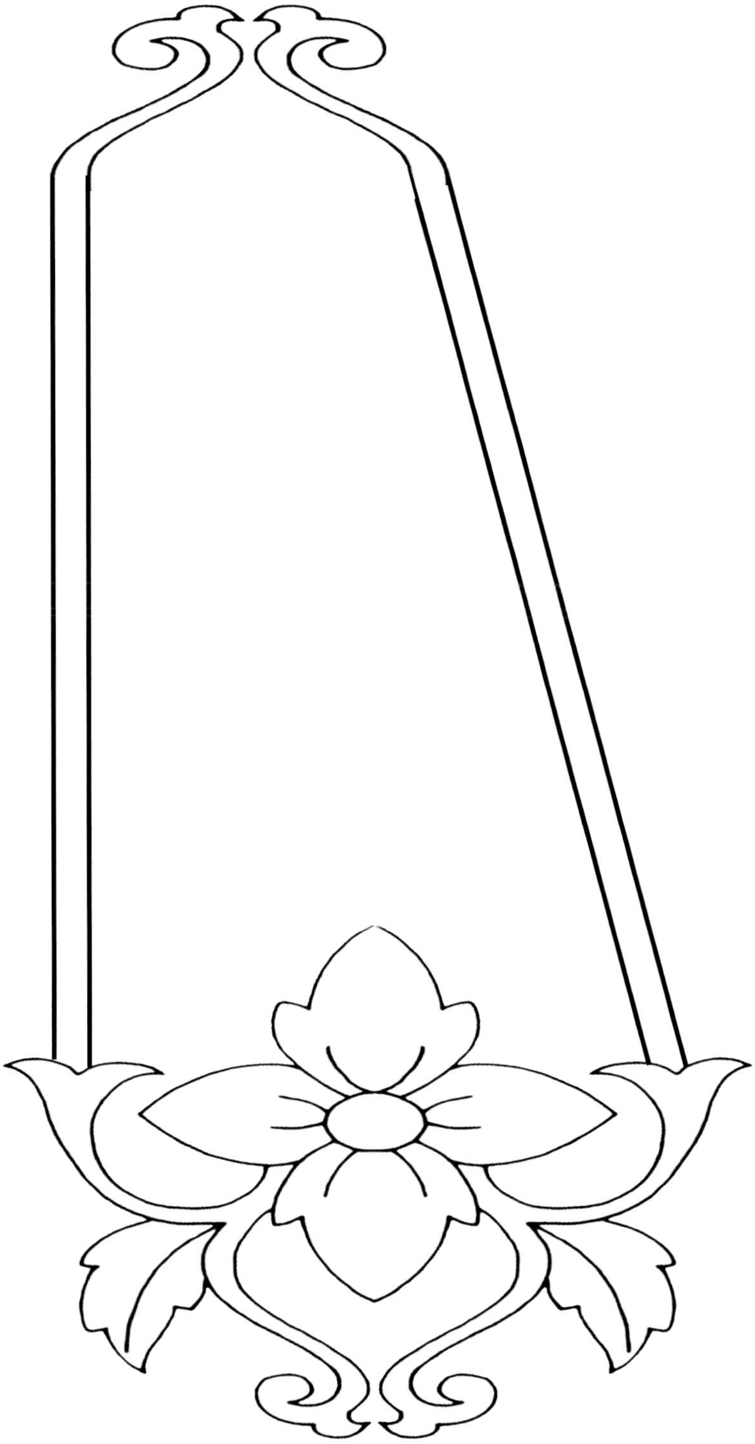

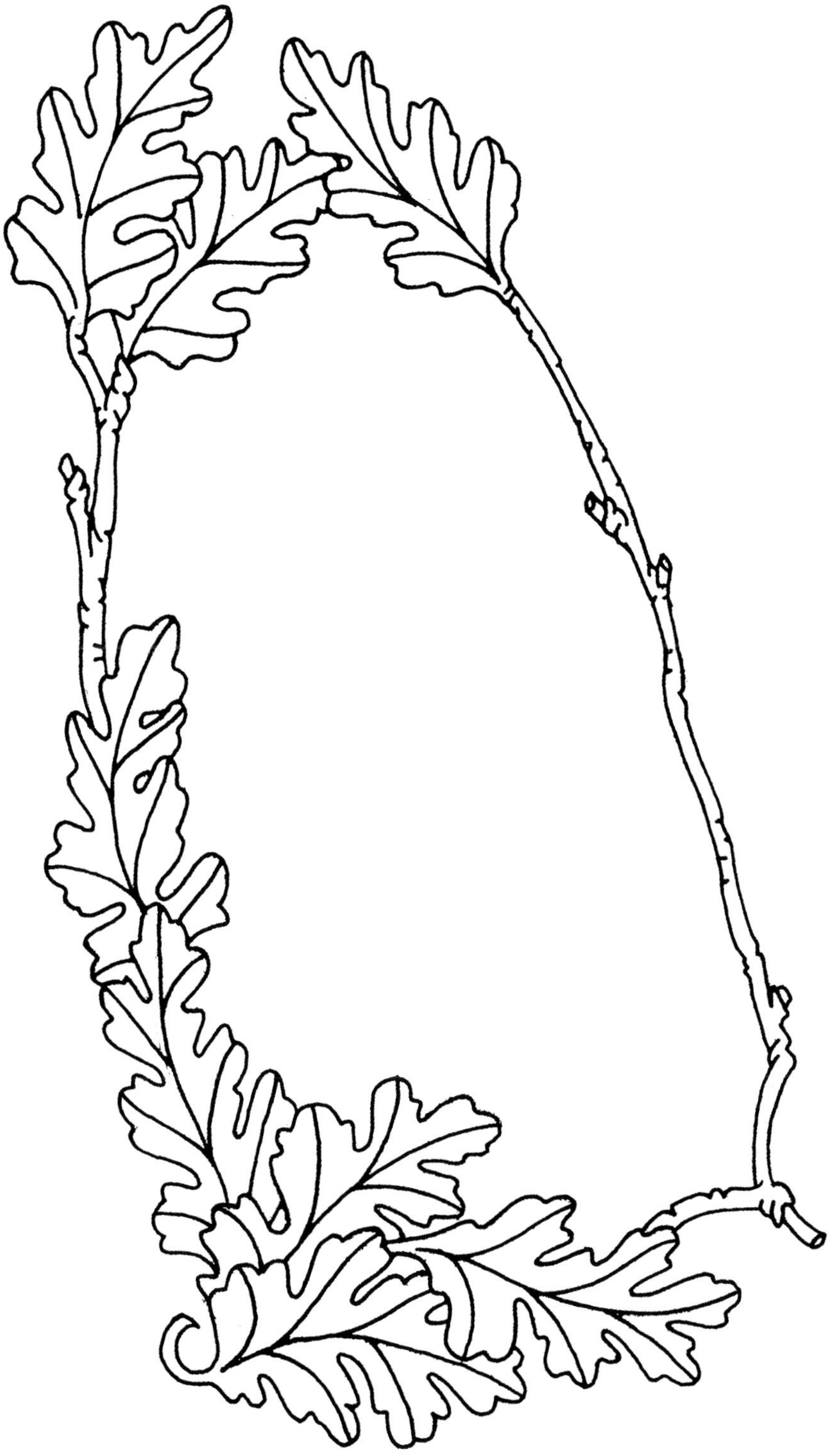

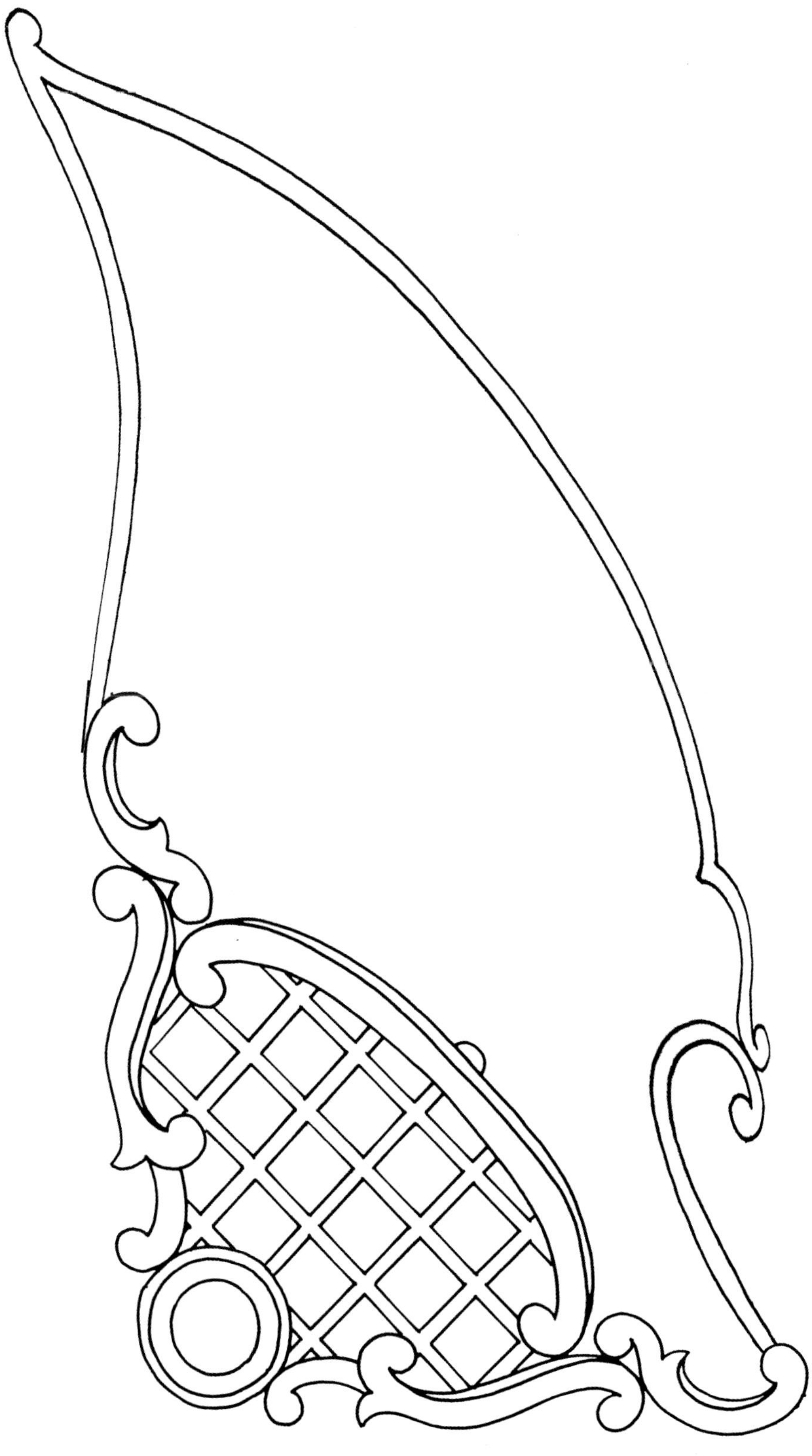

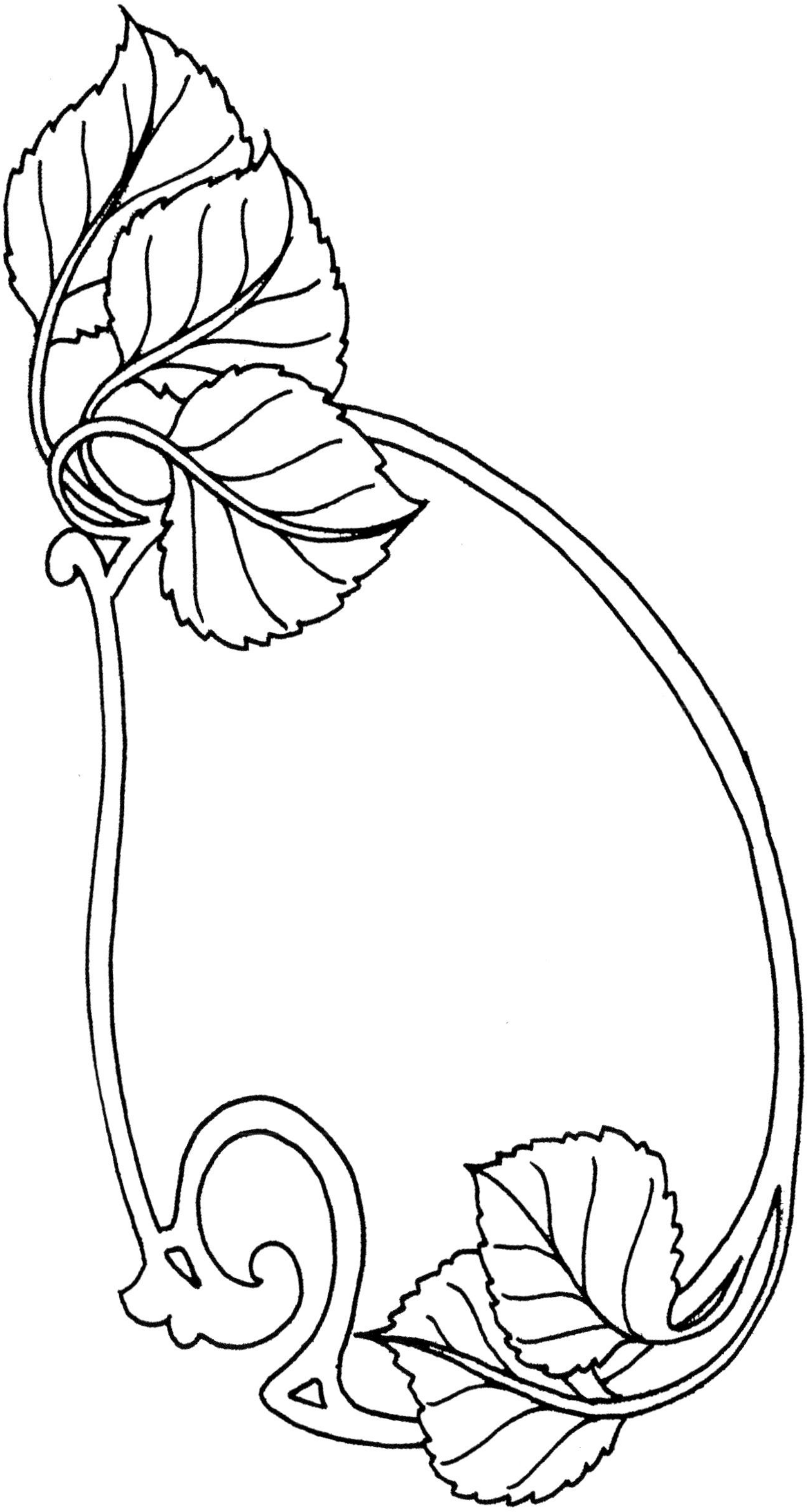

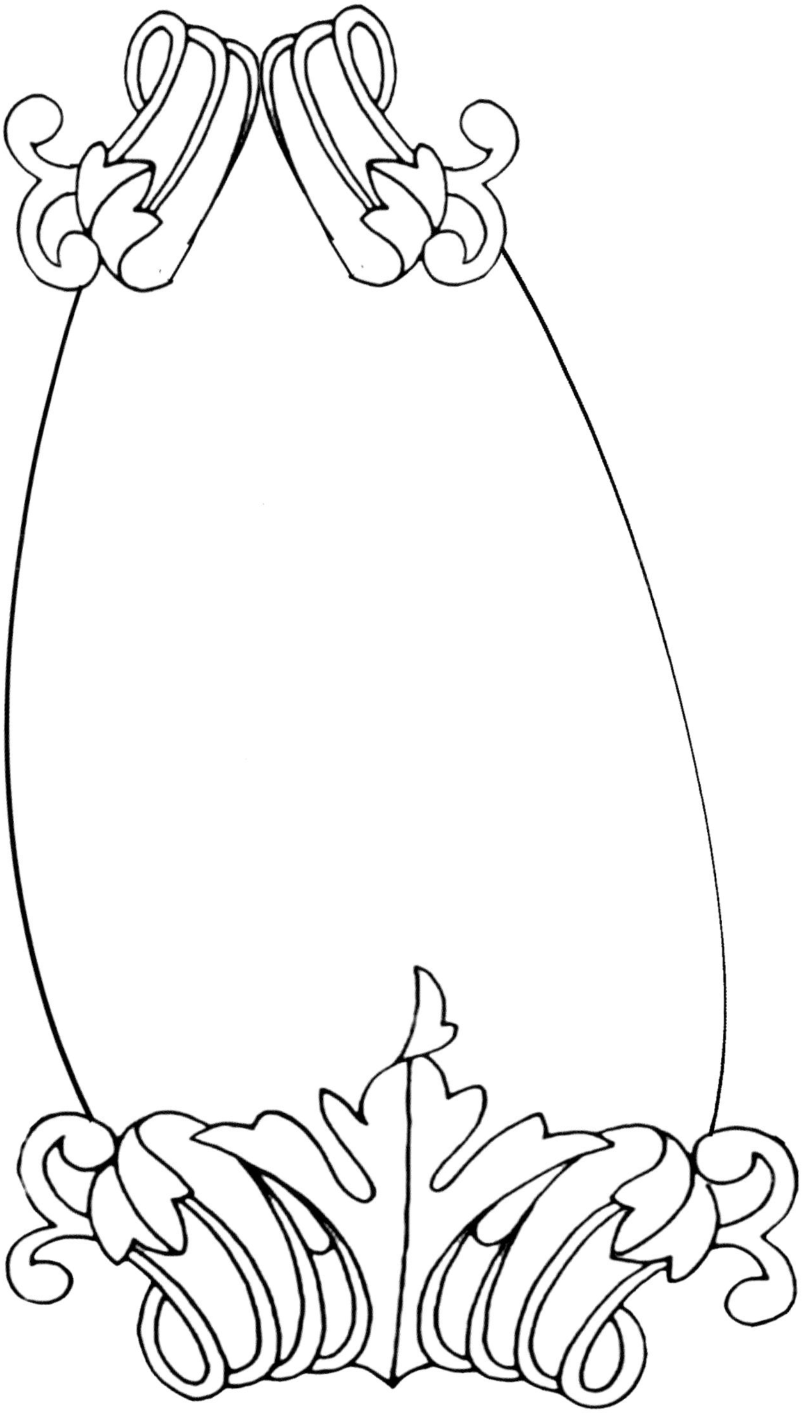

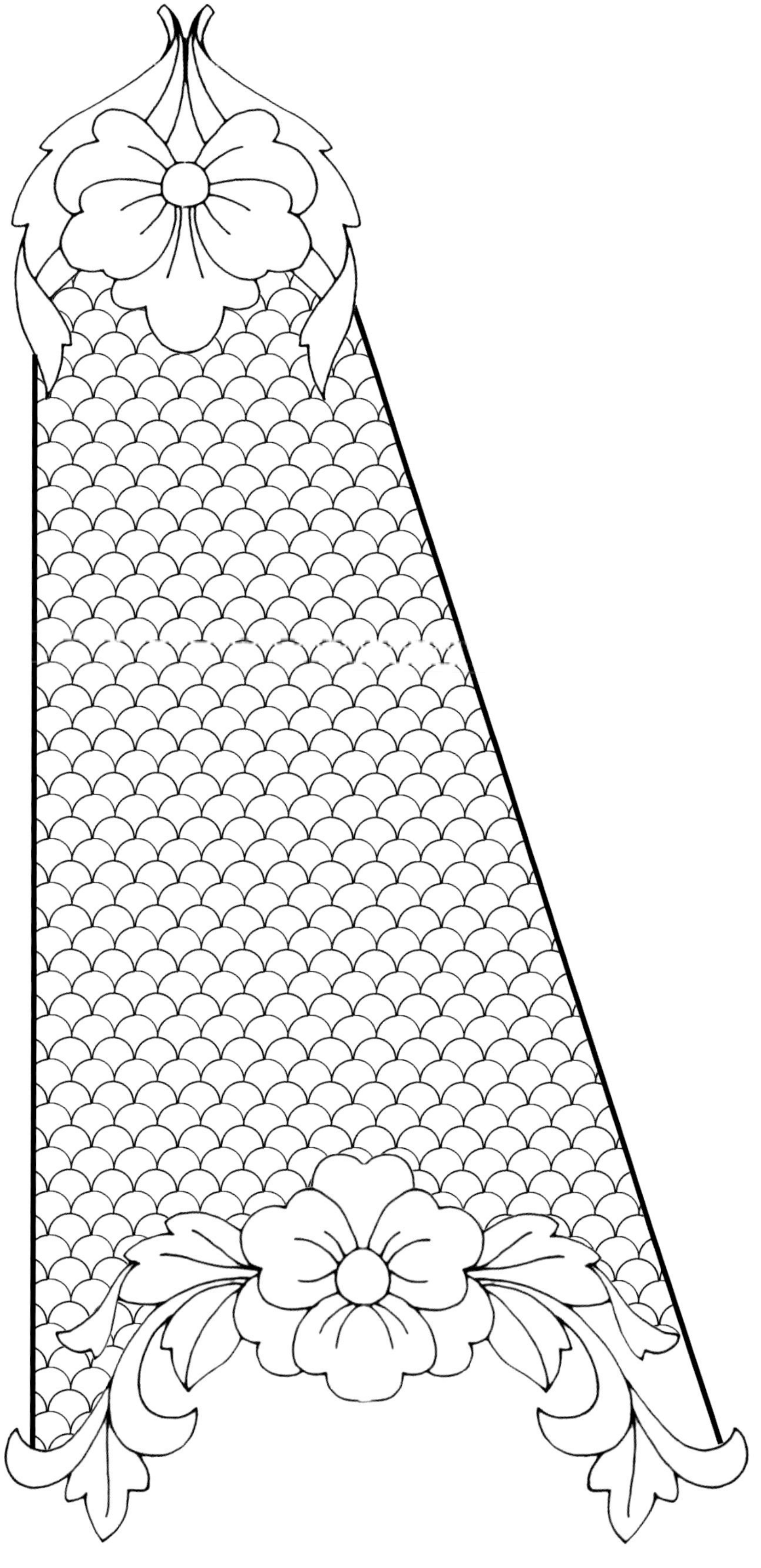

Checkering Blueprints

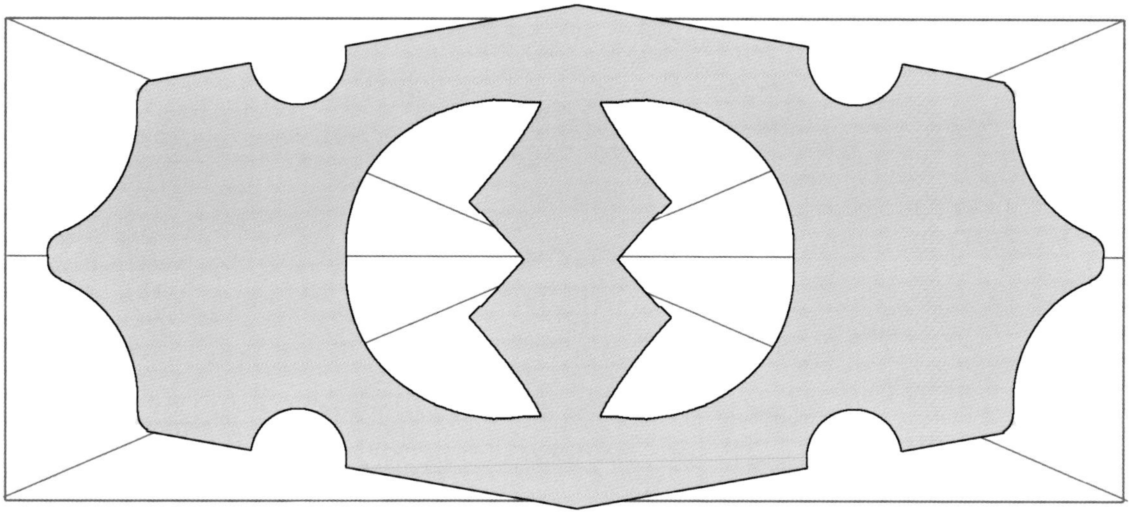

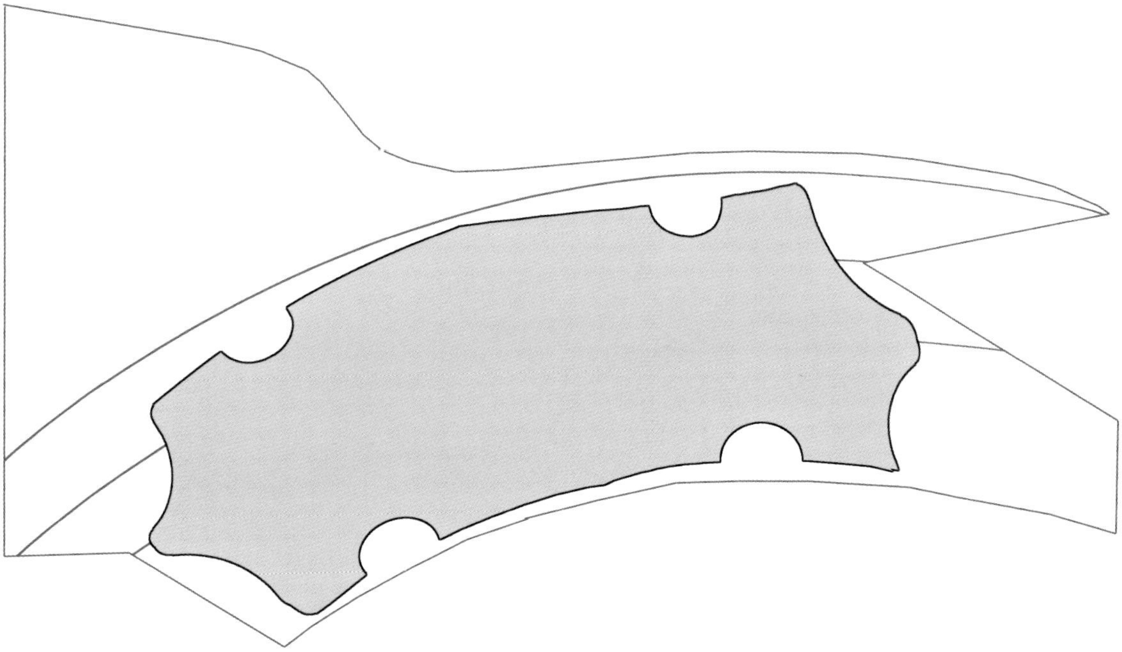

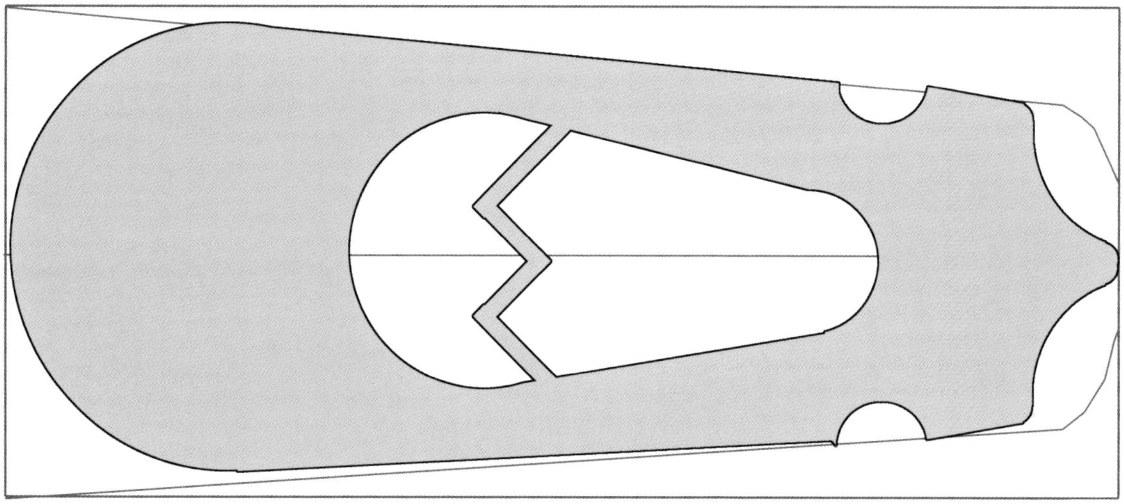

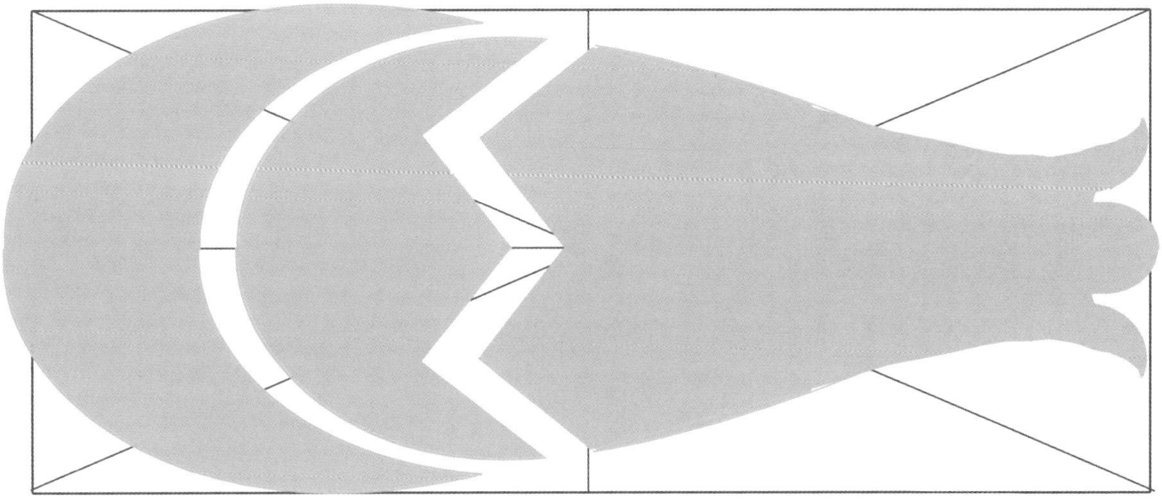

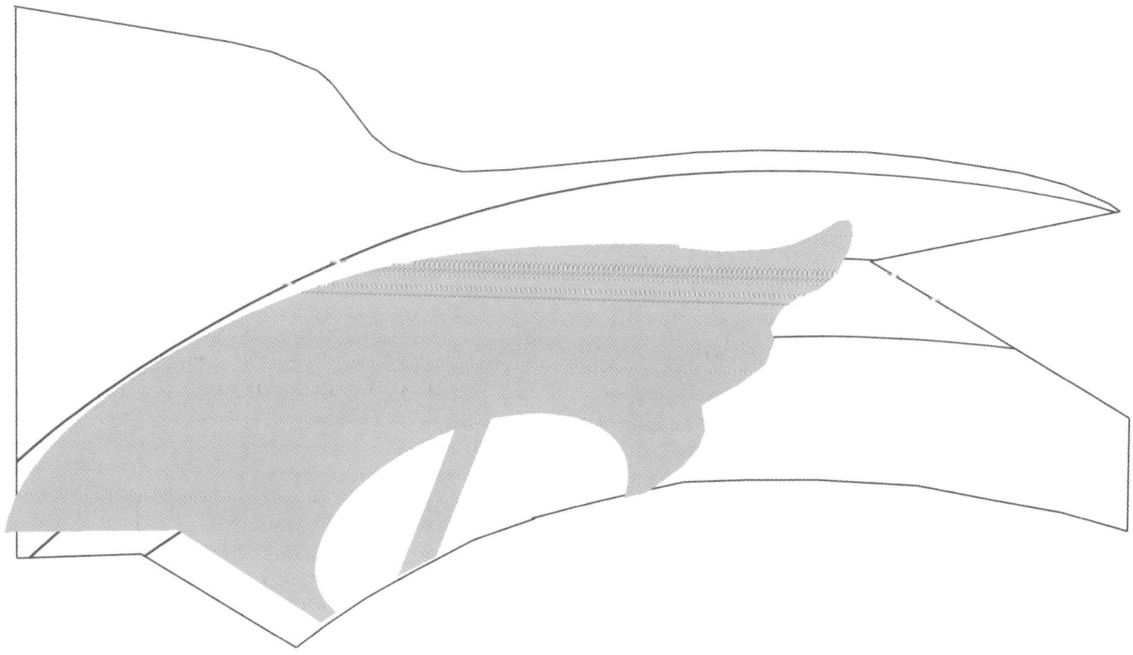

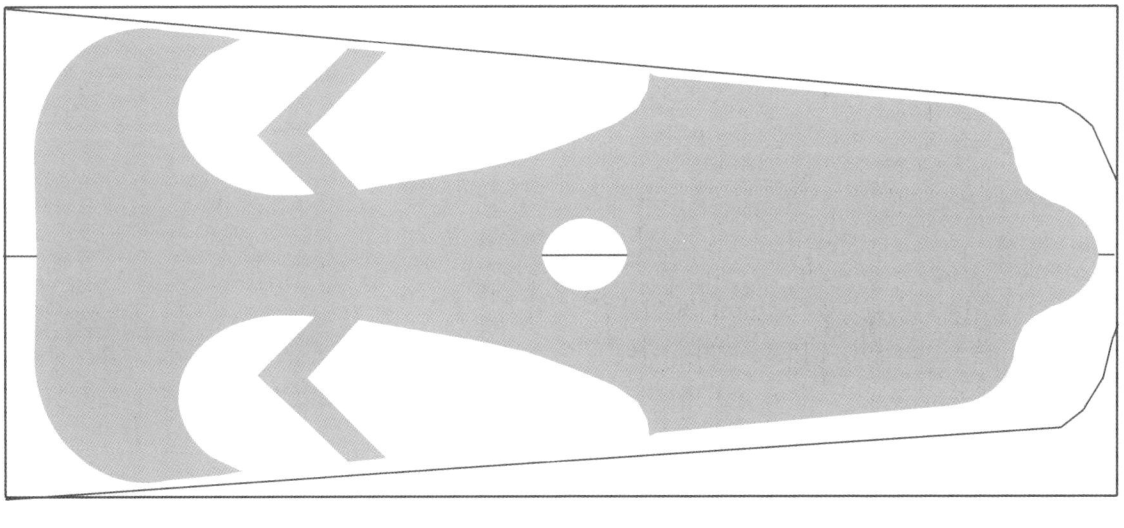

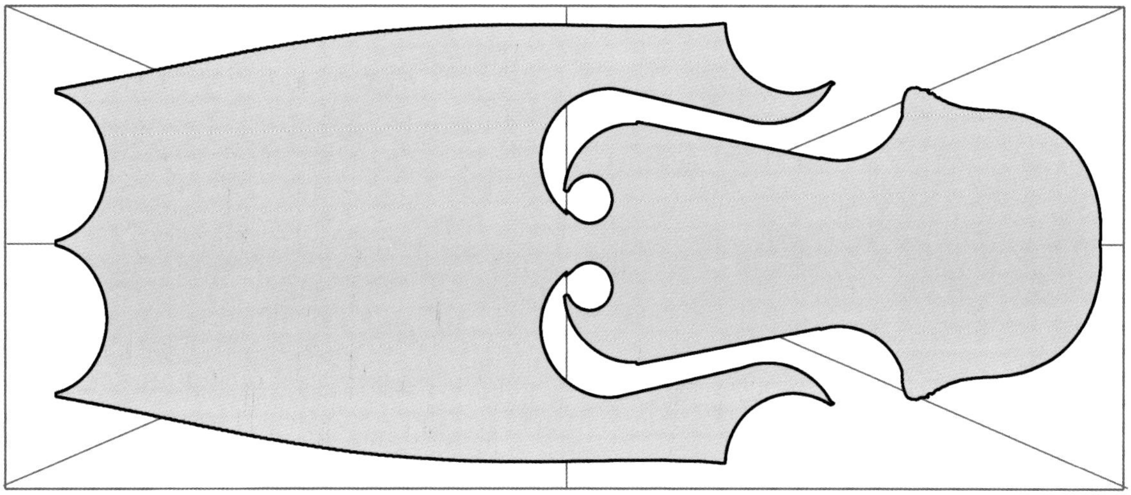

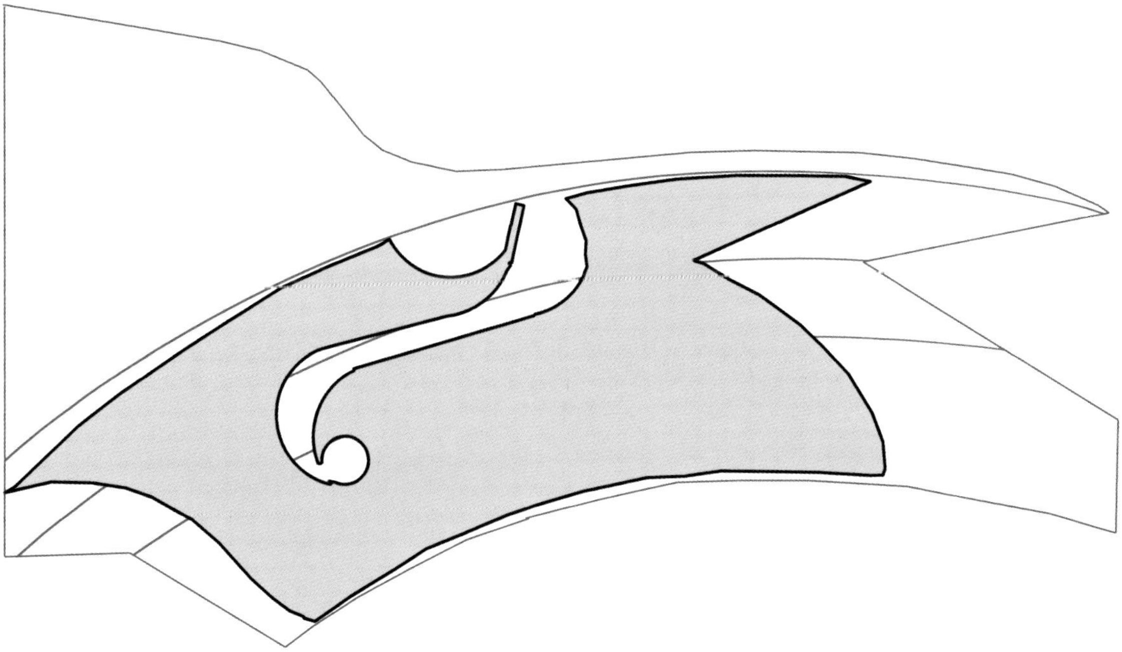

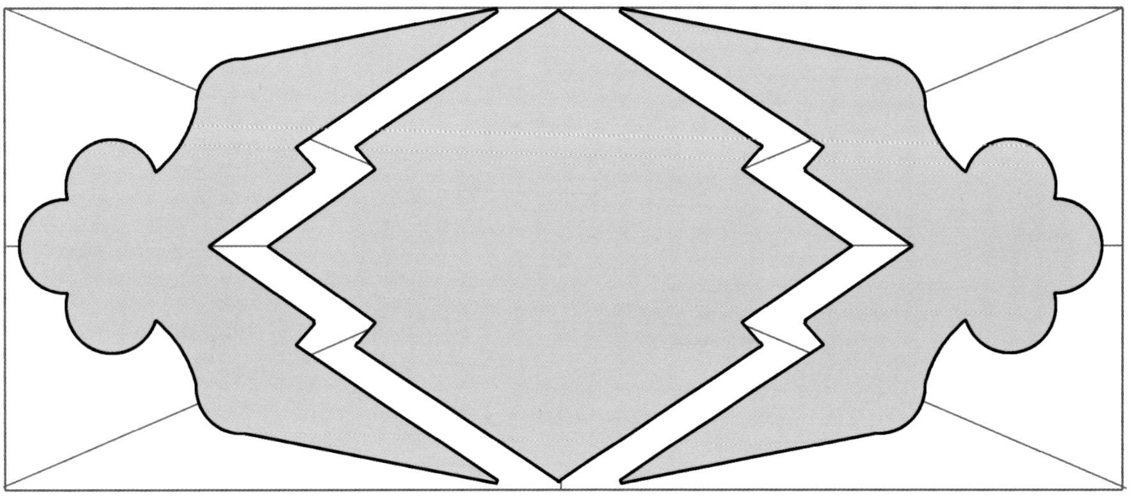

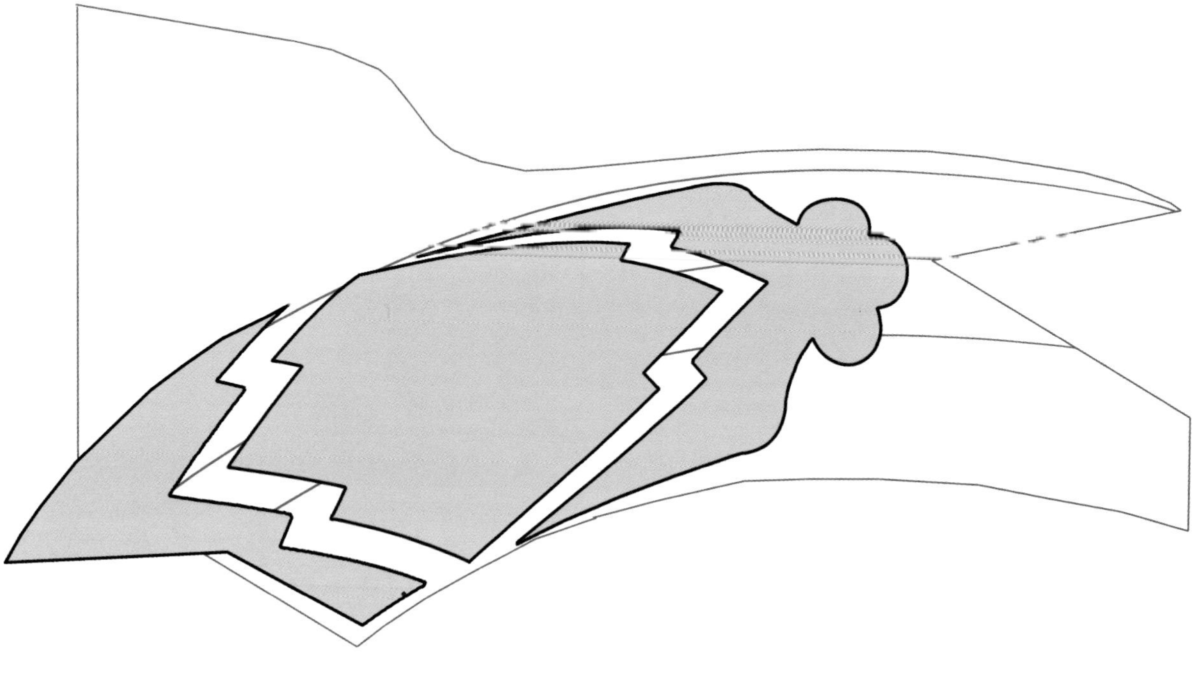

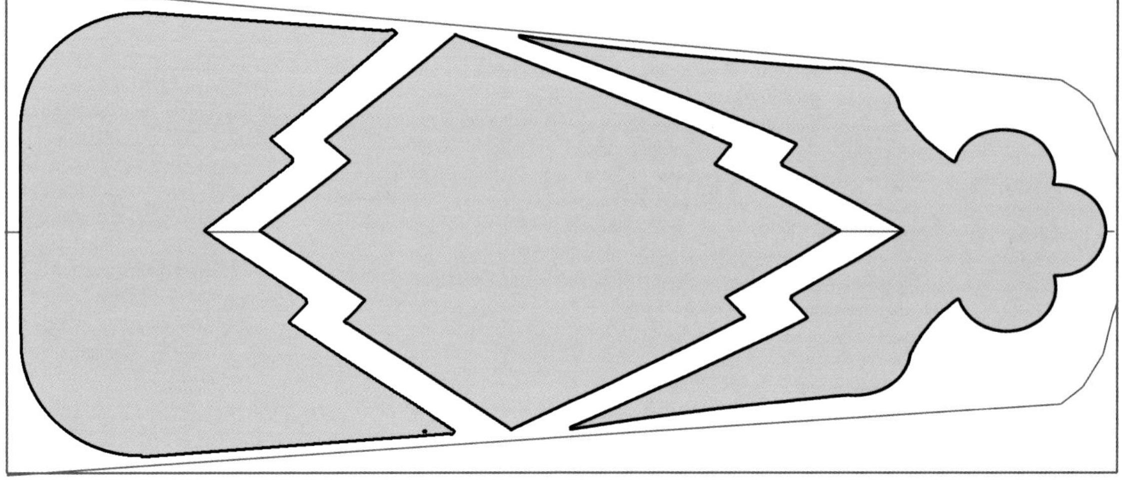

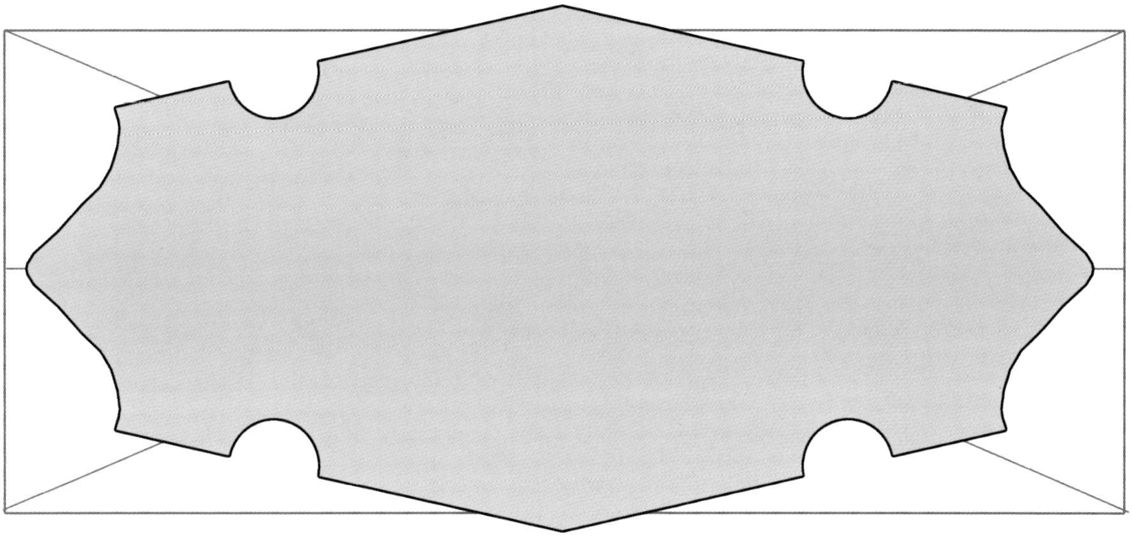

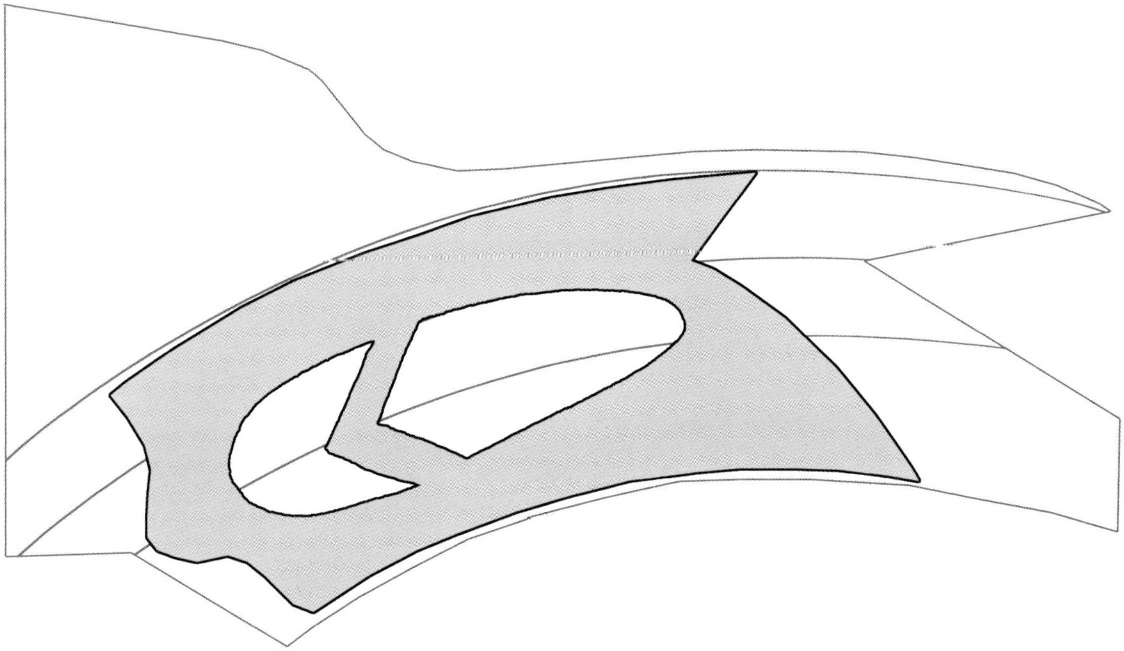

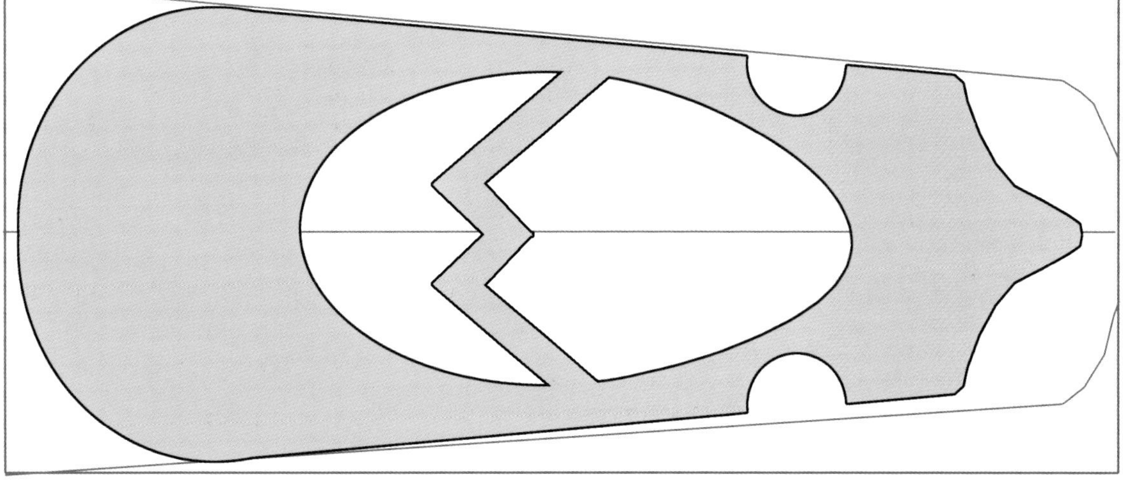

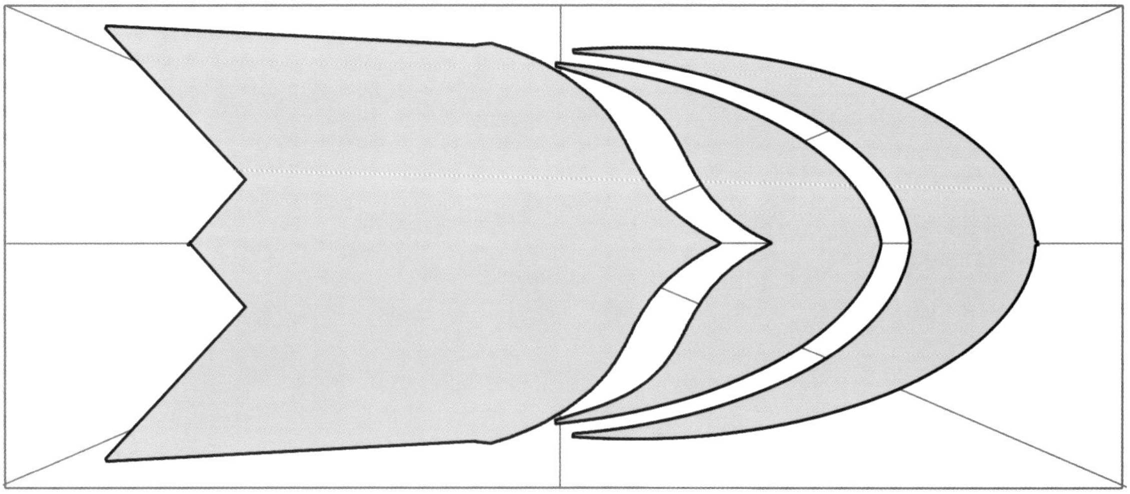

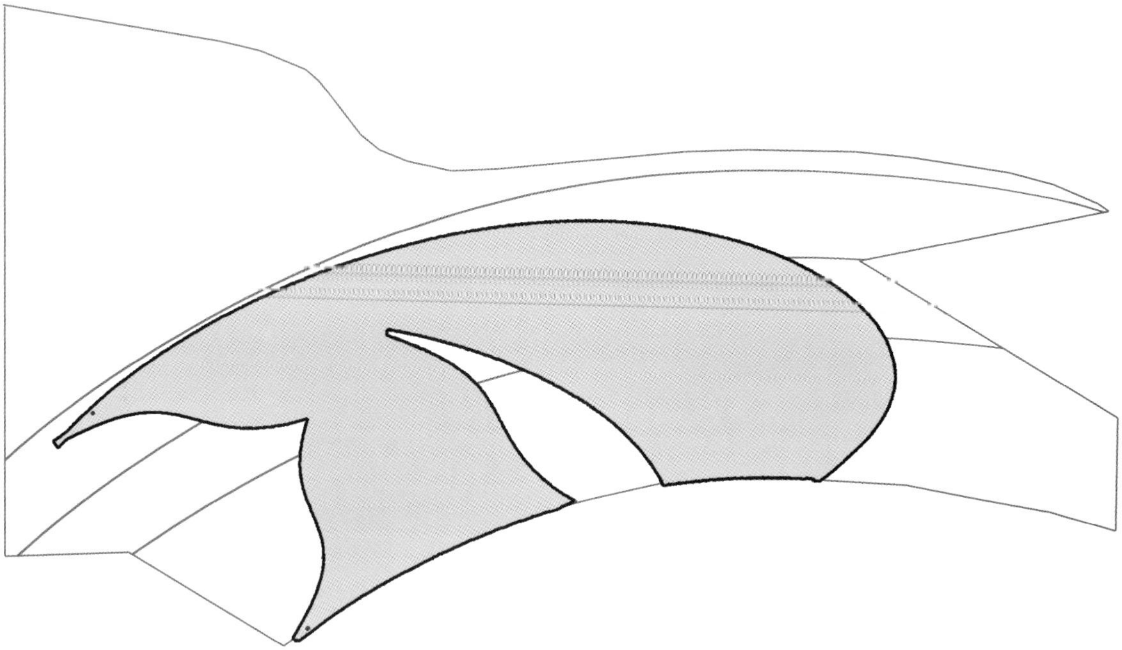

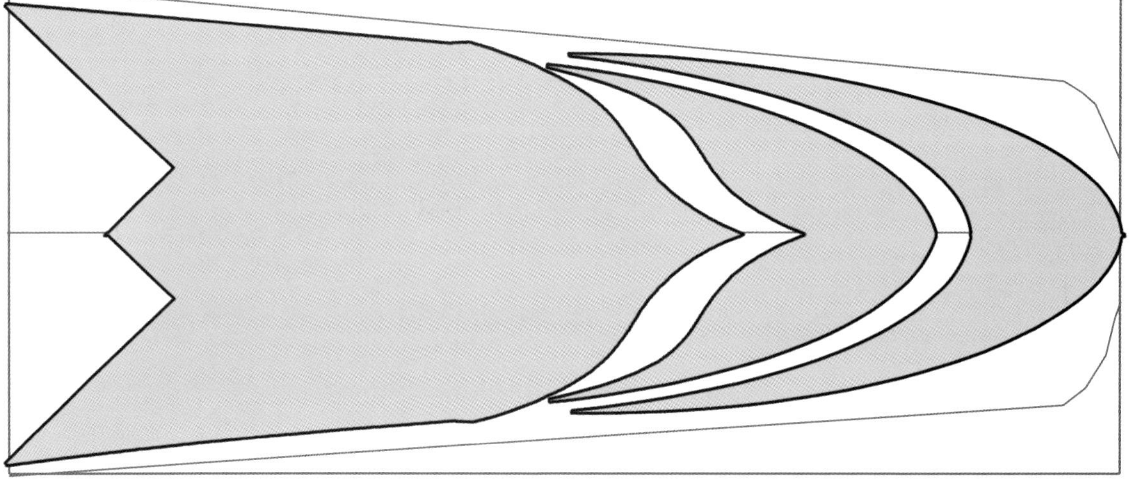

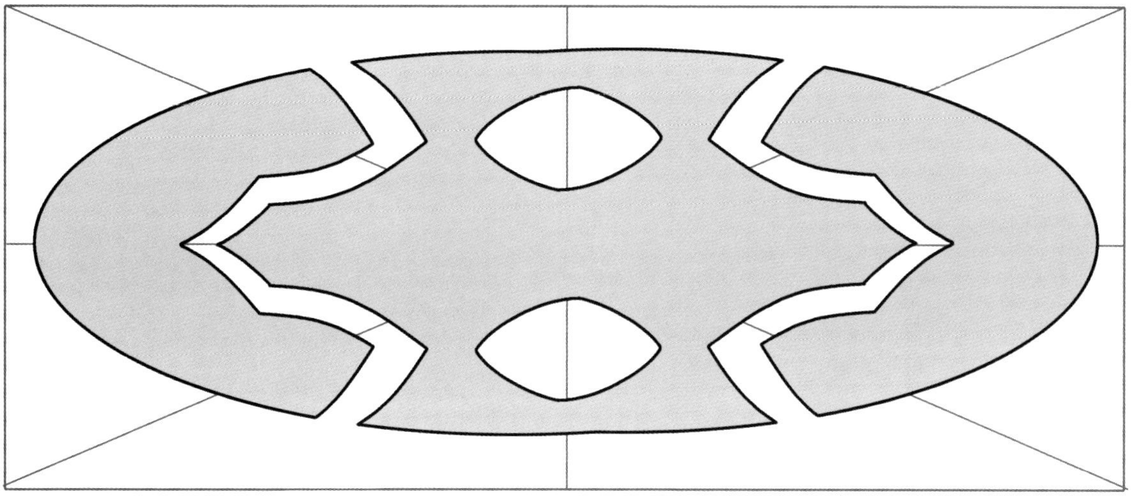

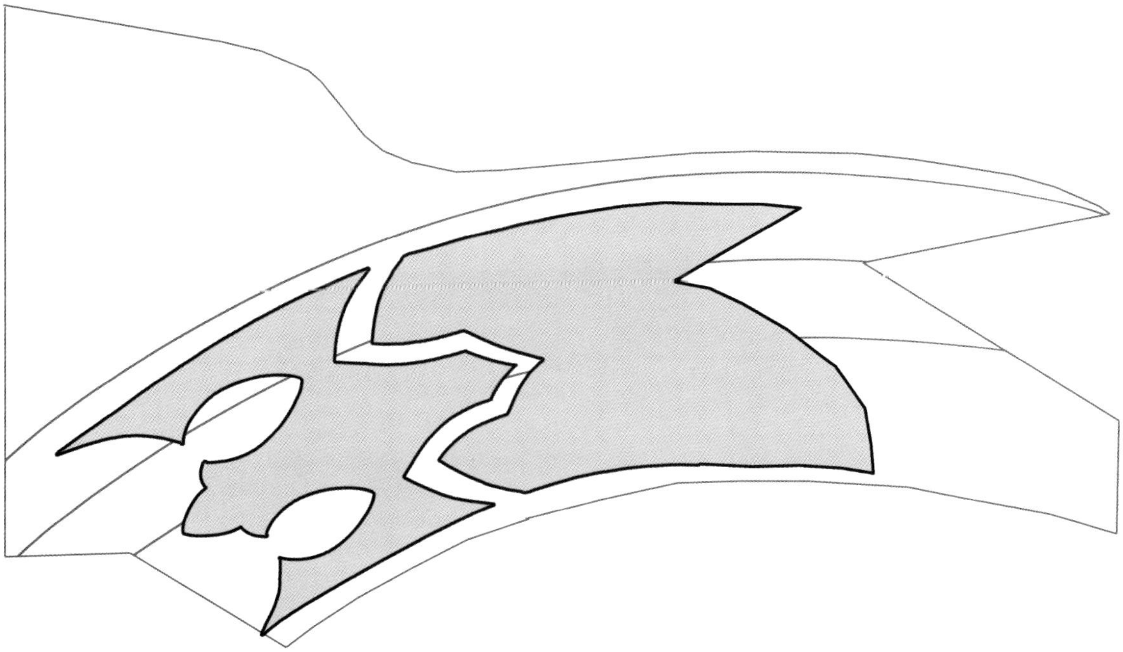

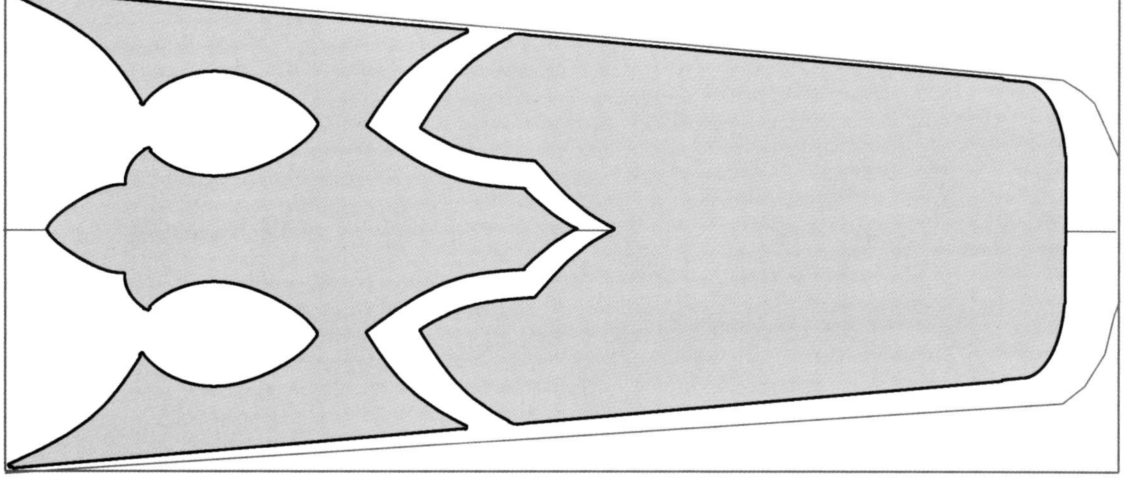

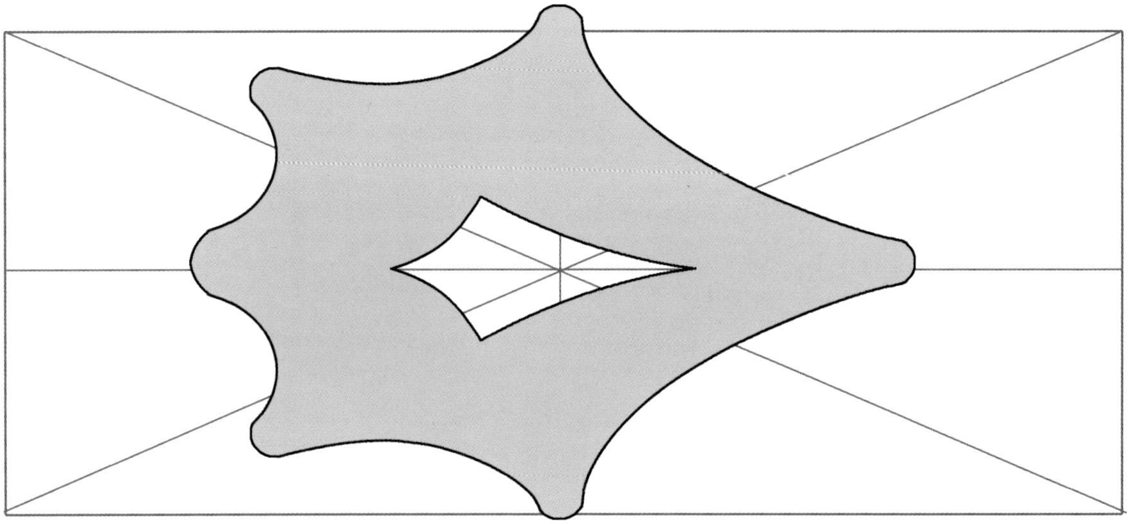

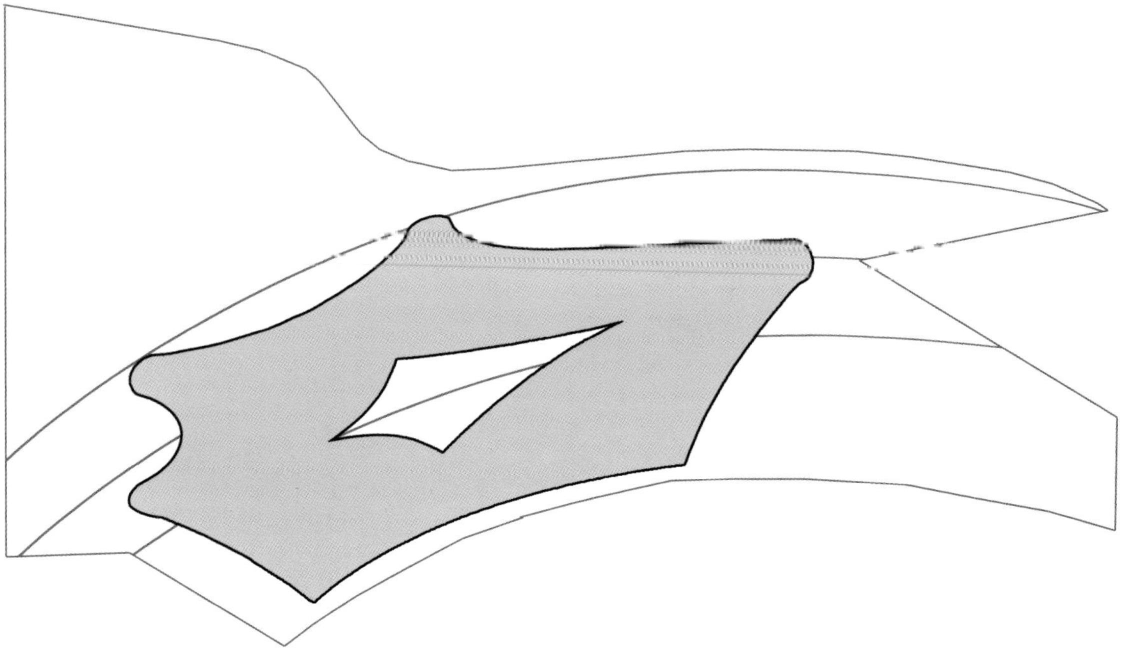

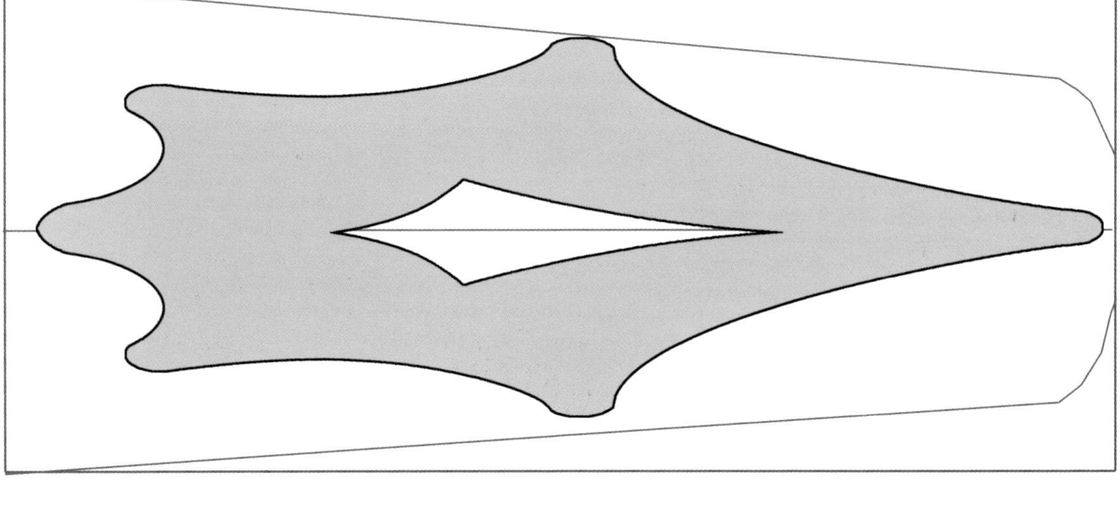

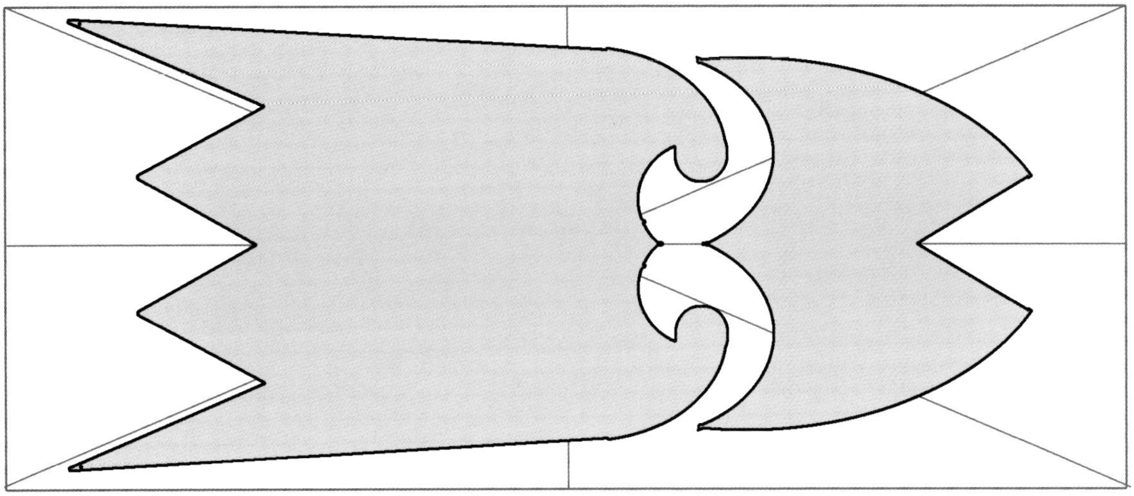

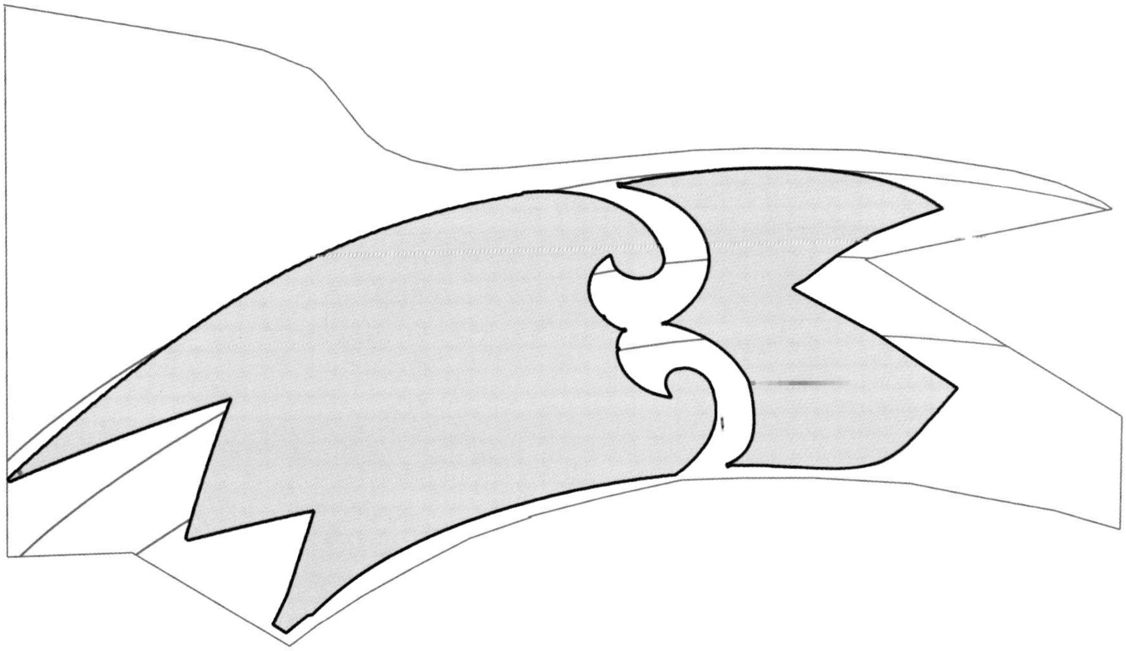

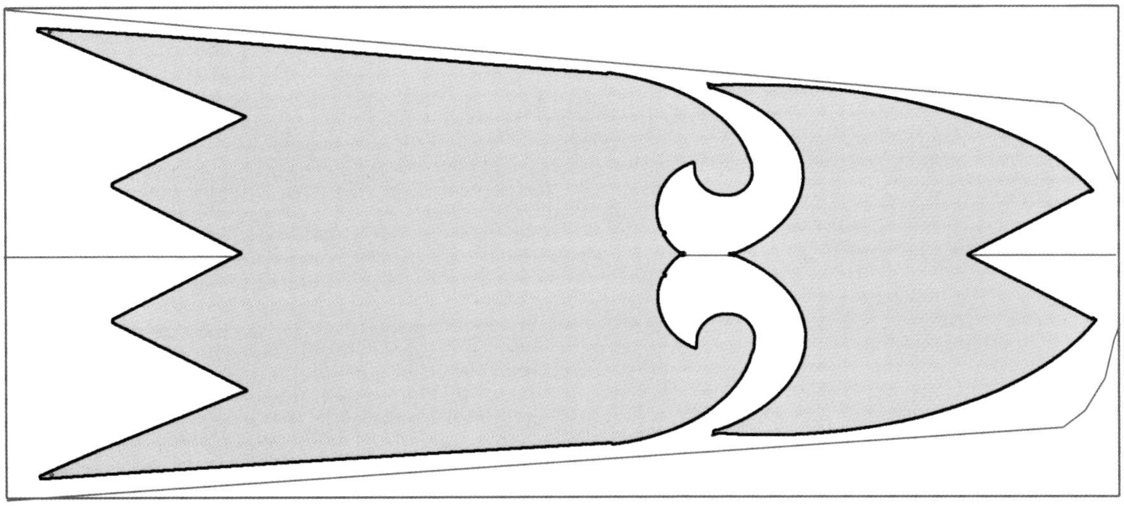

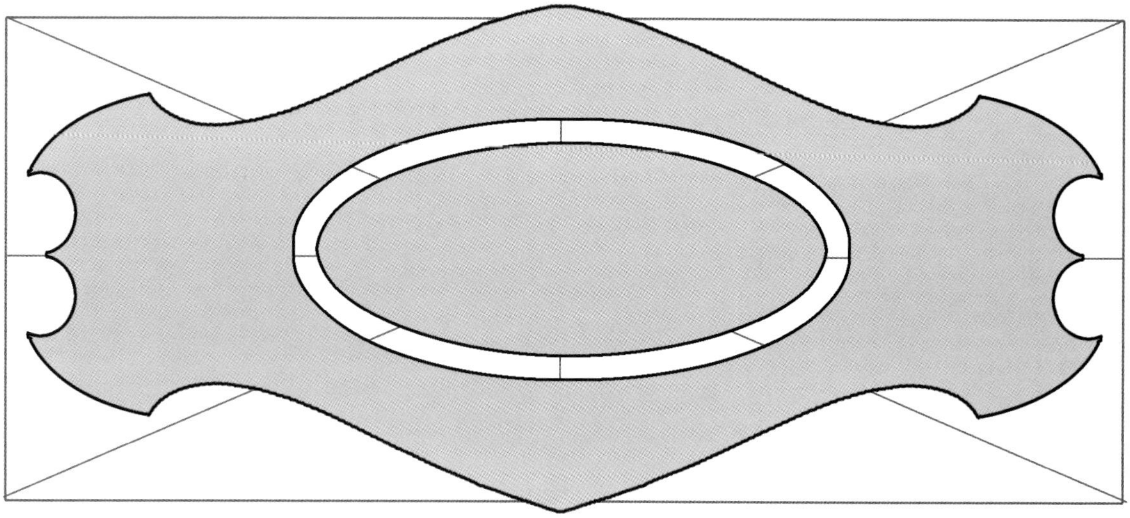

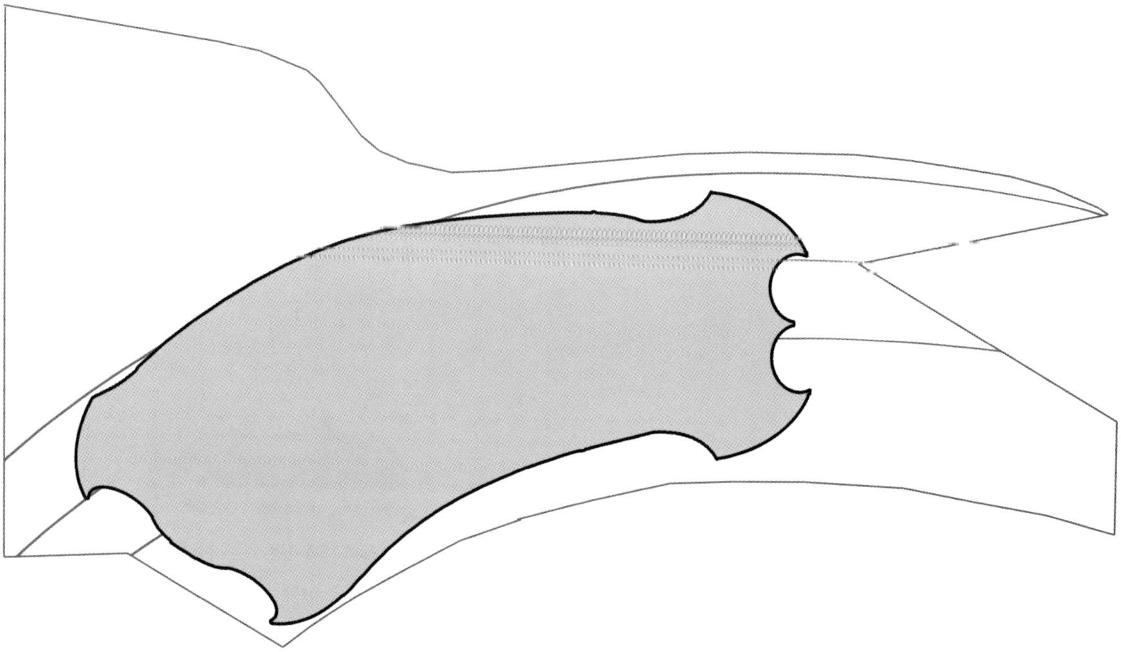

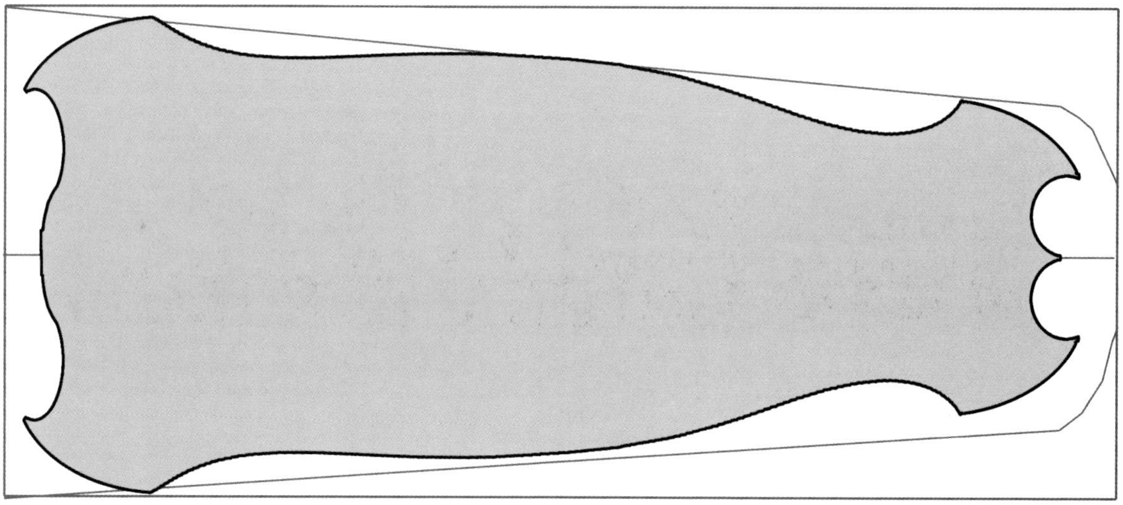

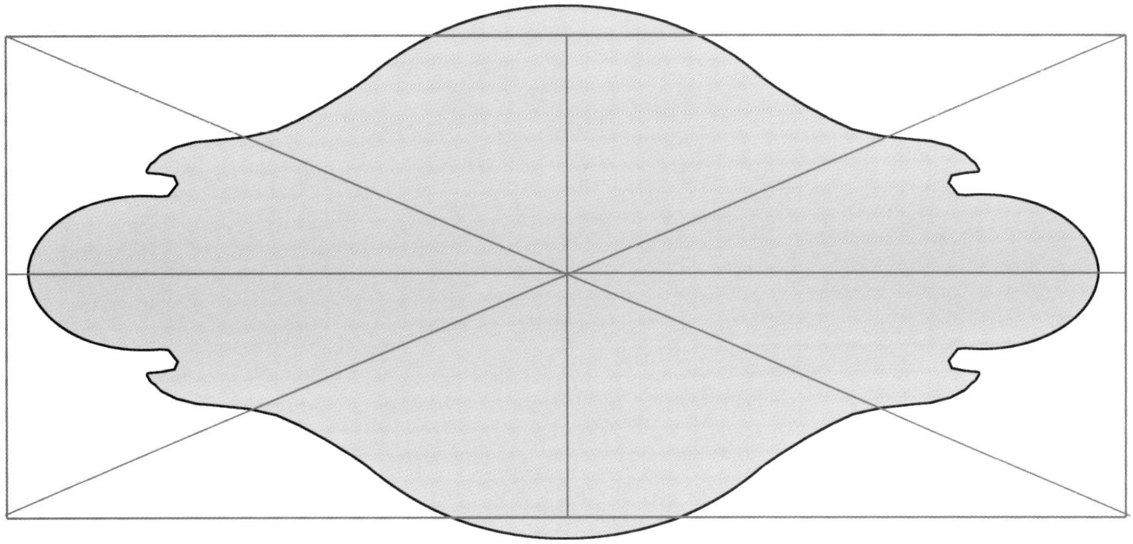

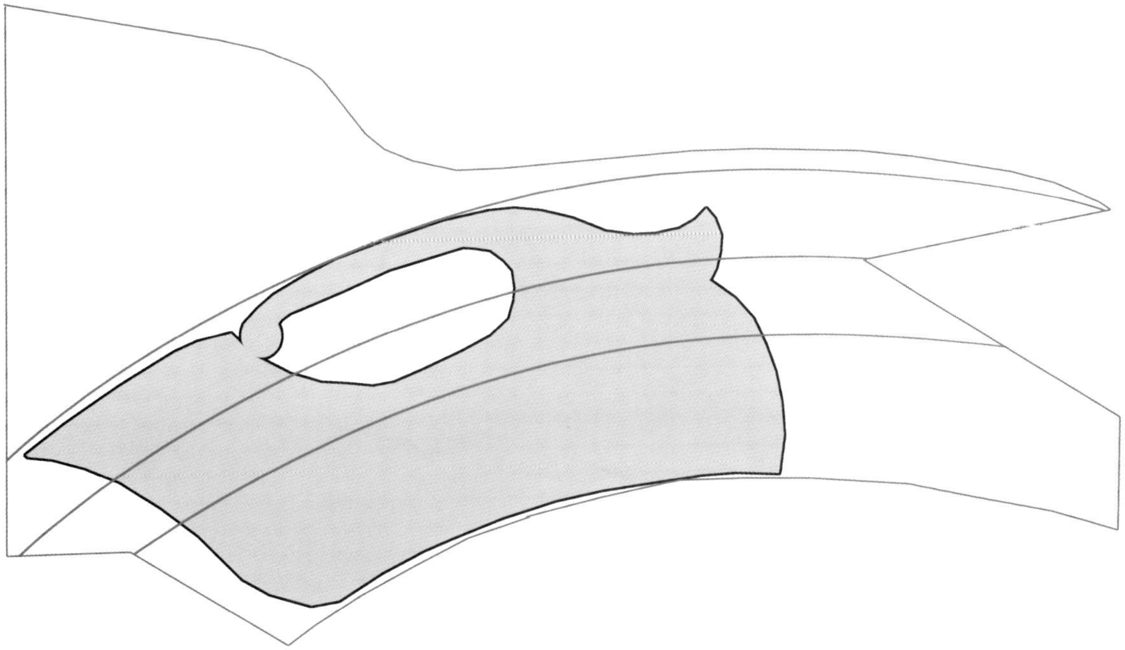

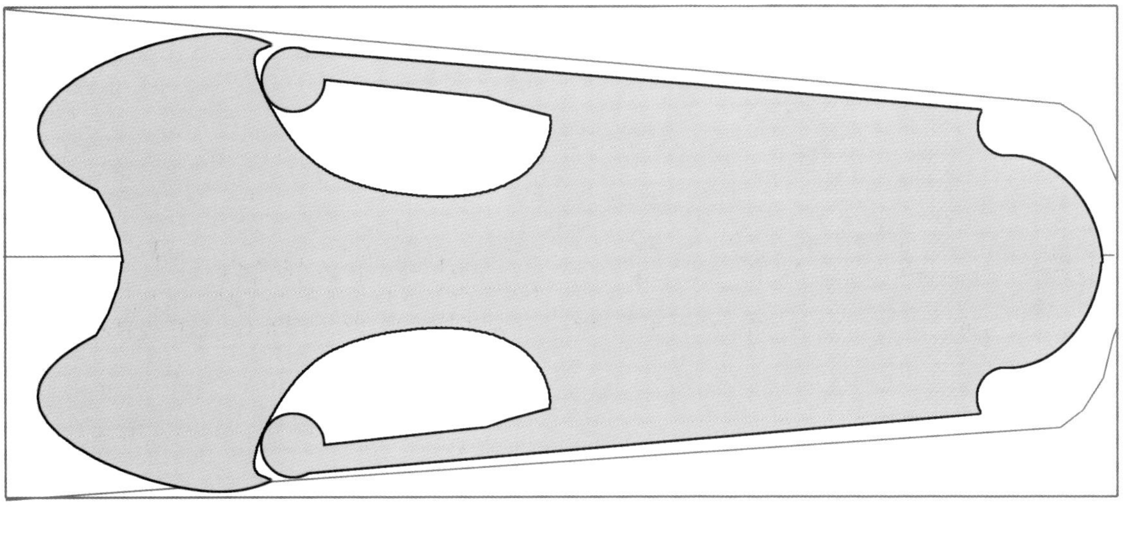

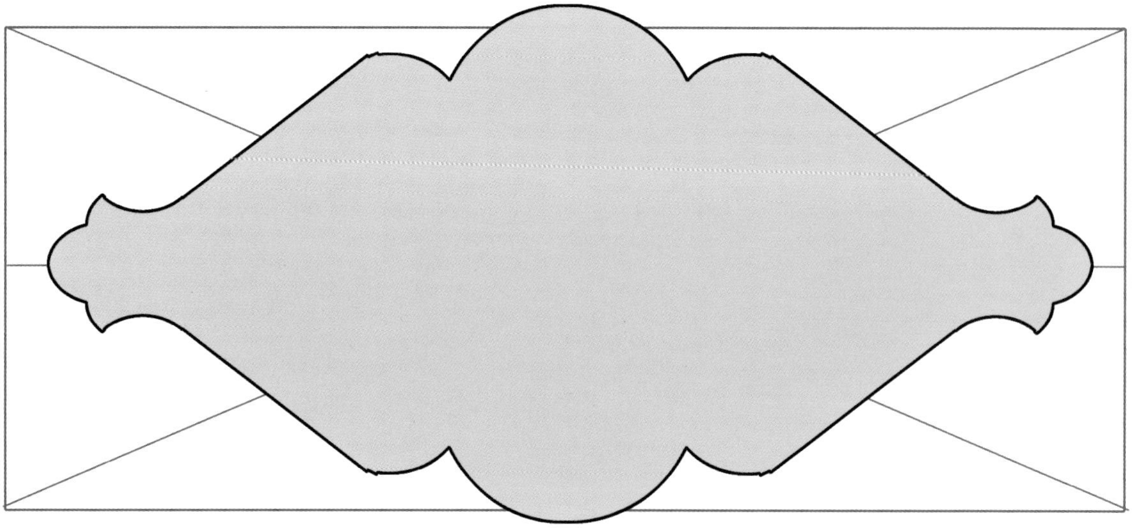

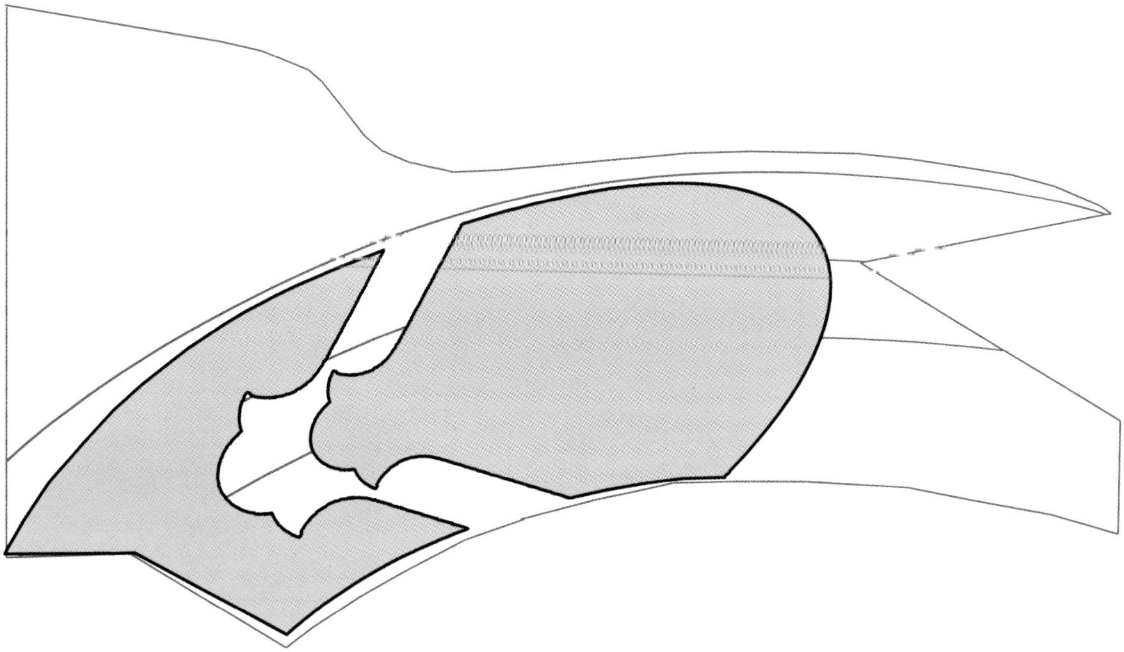

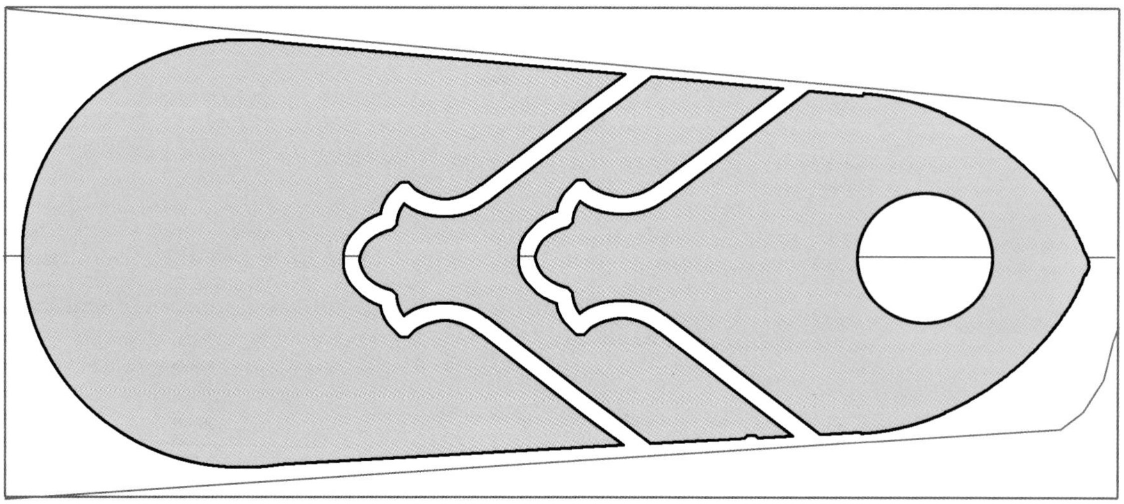

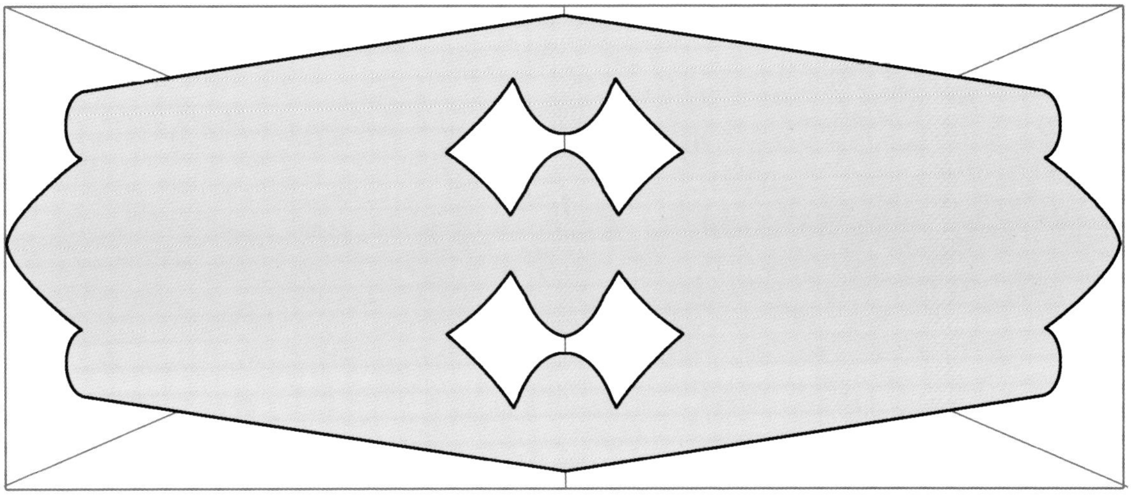

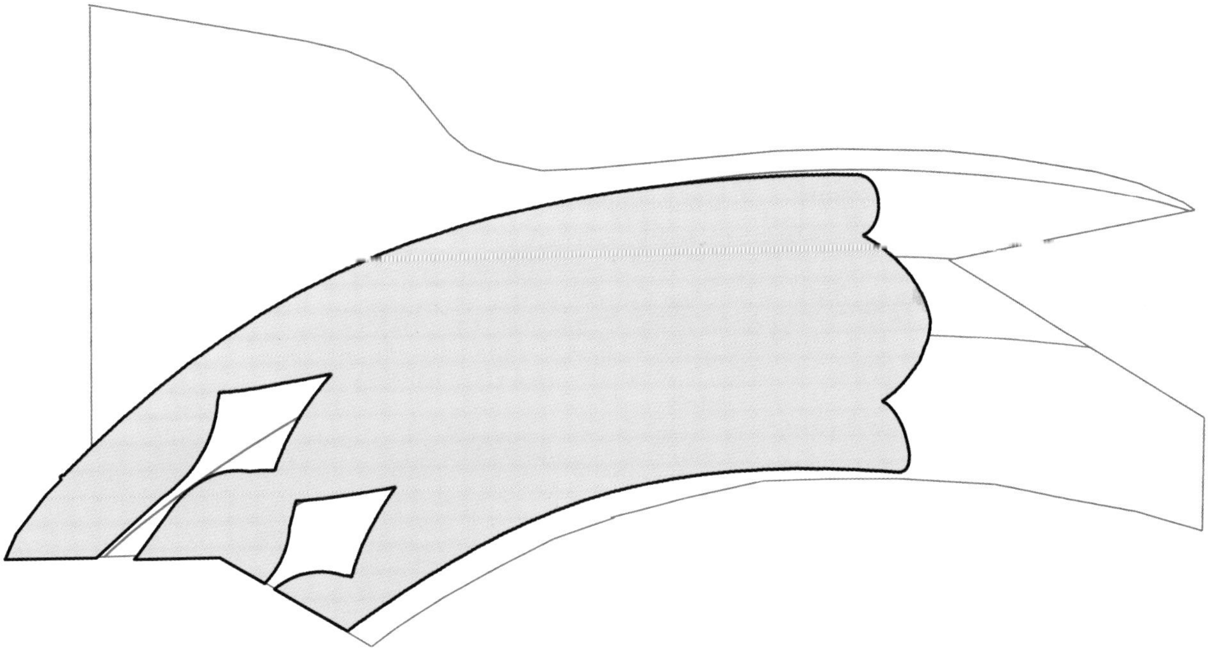

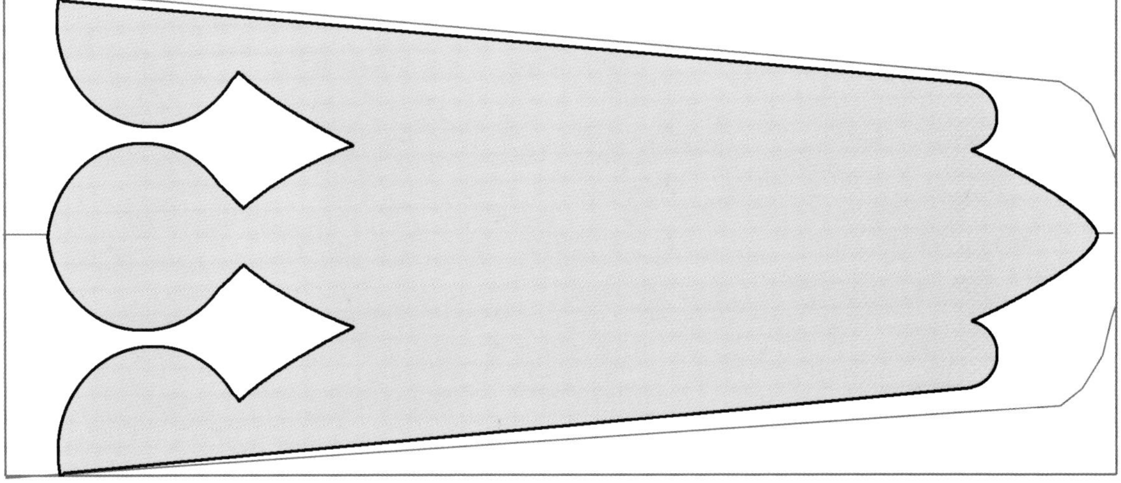

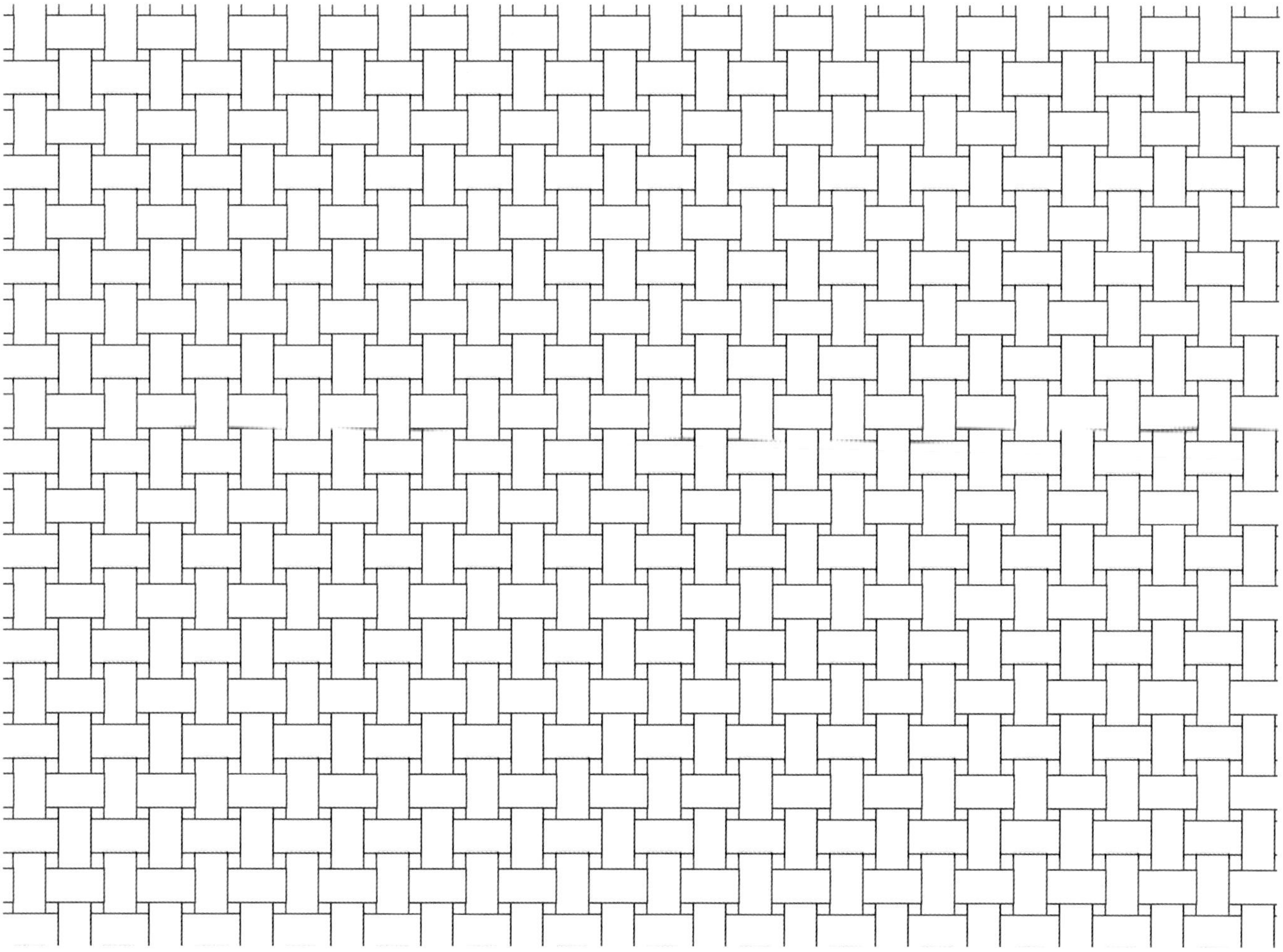

Stock Templates

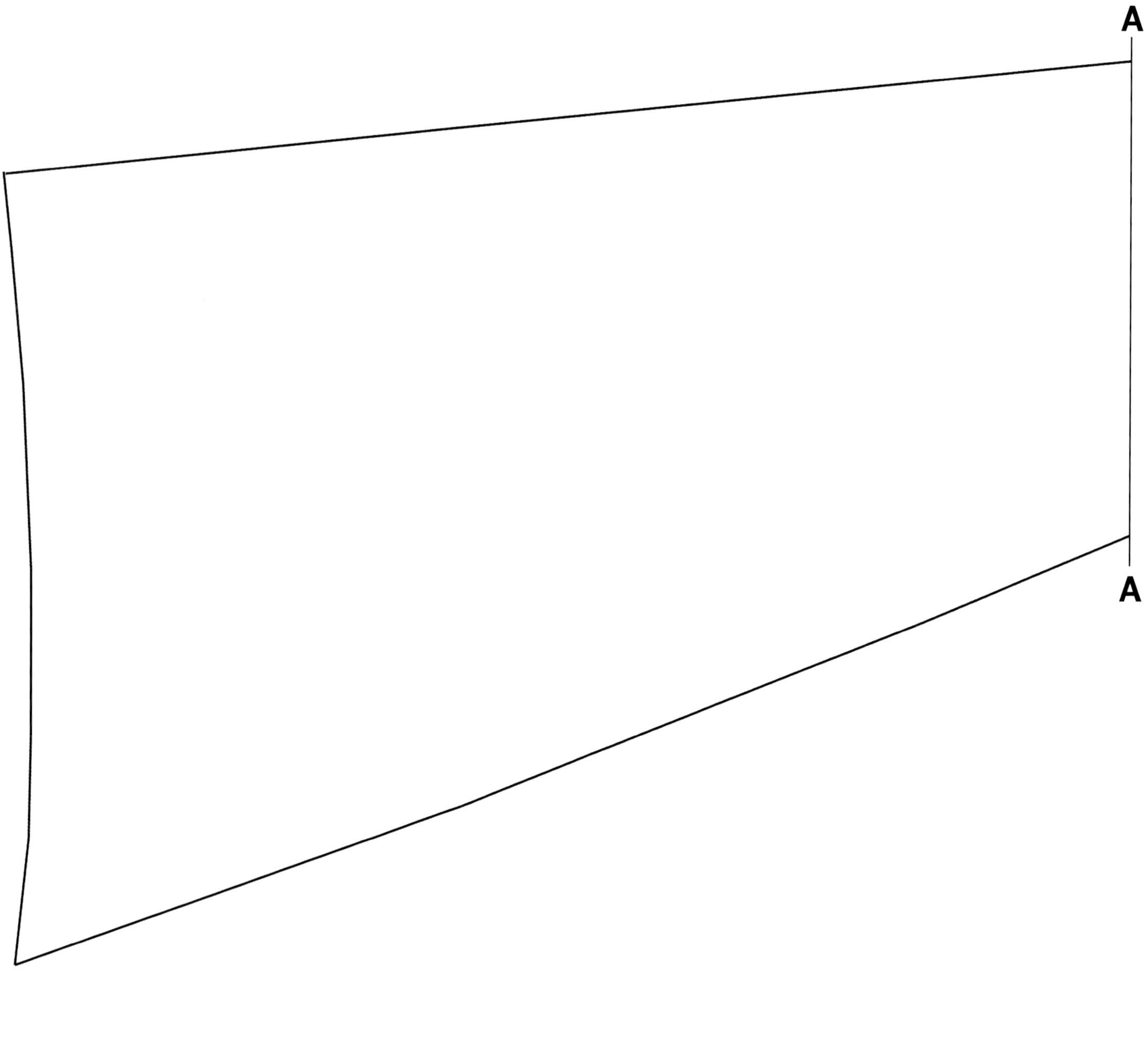

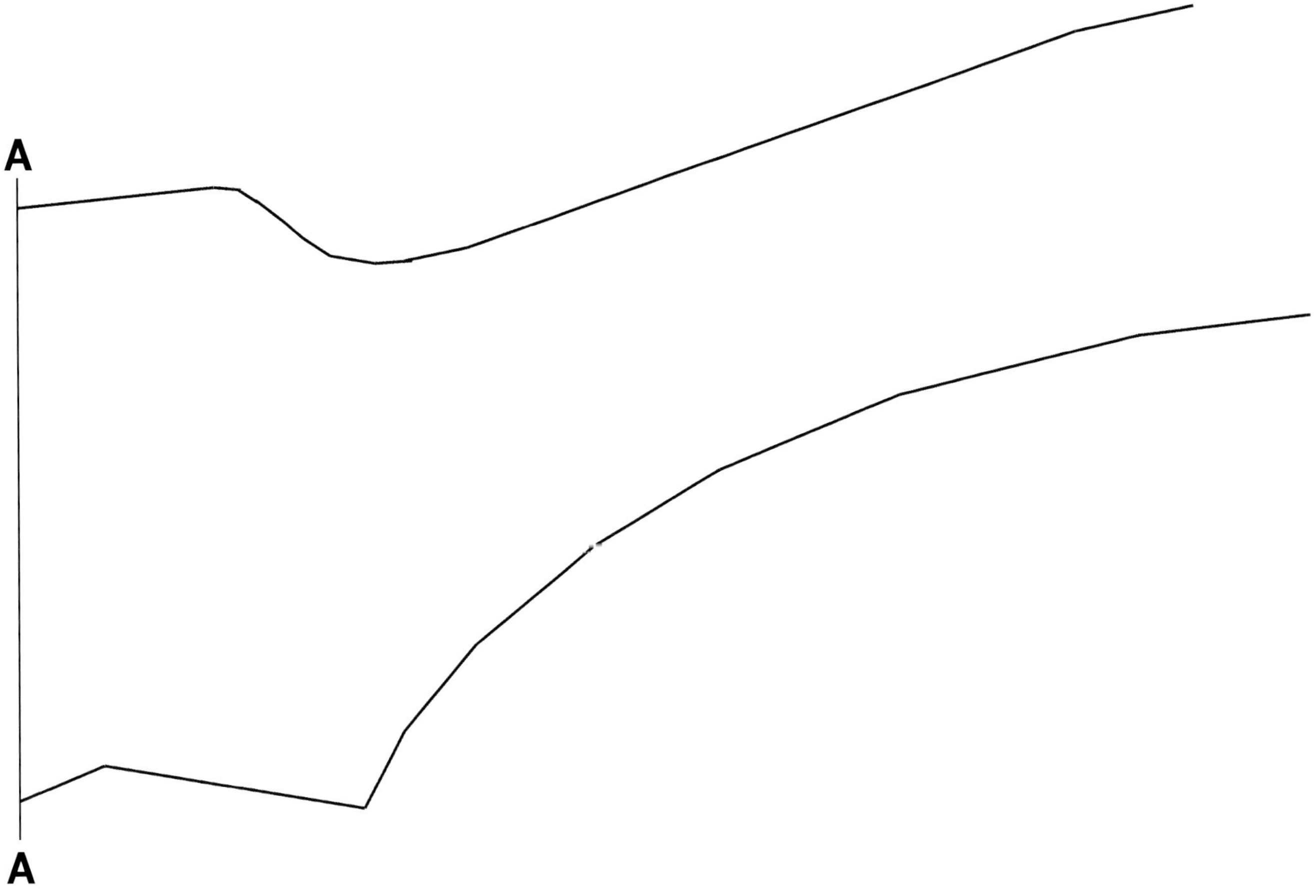
A
A

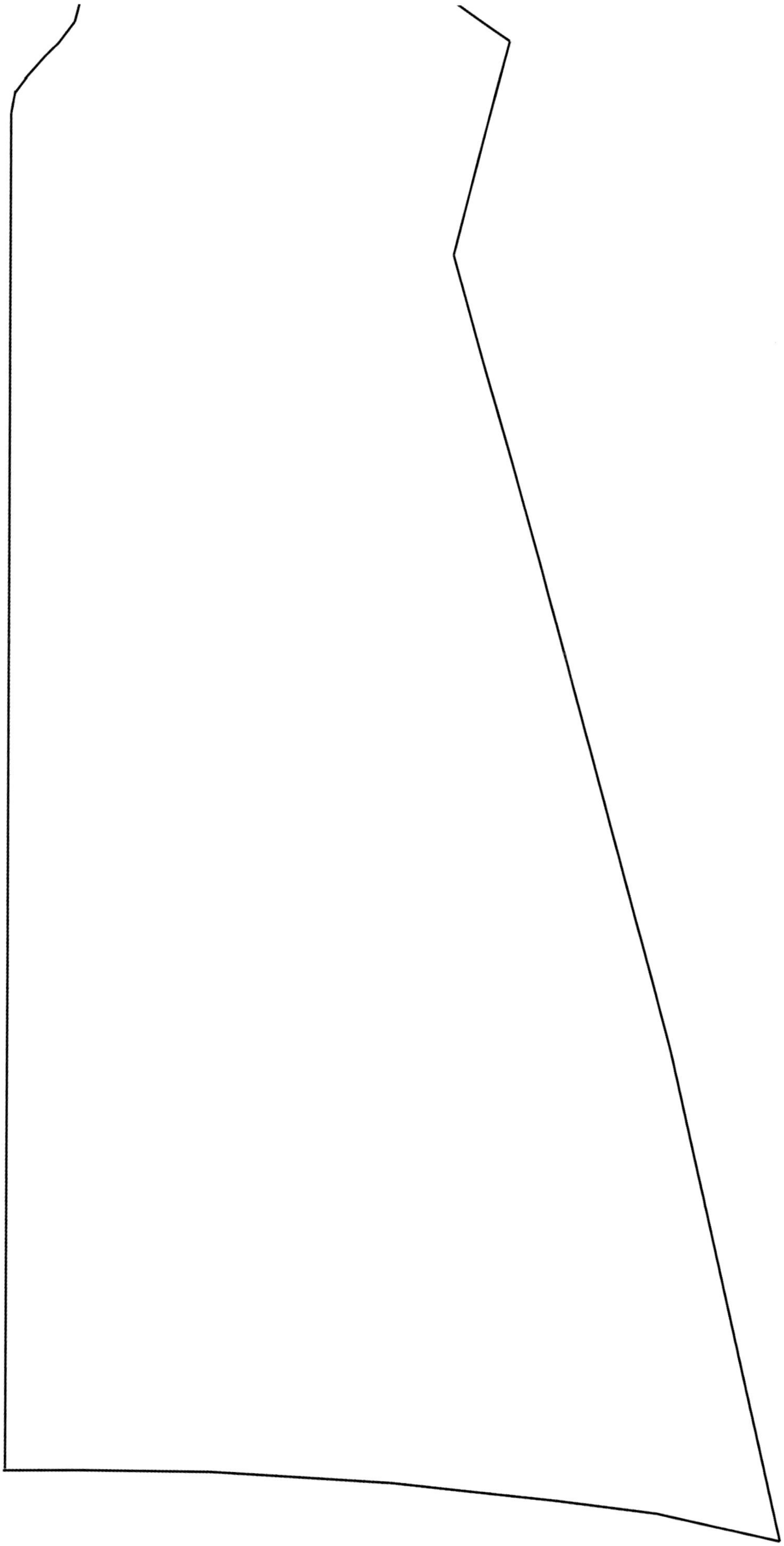

Index

Note: Page numbers in *italics* indicate patterns, blueprints, and templates.

A

altering patterns, 8
animal patterns, *18–32*. *See also* bird and waterfowl patterns
- bears, *18, 27*
- bobcat and pintail, *30*
- buffalo, *25, 31*
- deer and elk, *18–24*
- fox and pheasant, *29*
- horse, *32*
- moose, *26*
- mountain goats and puma, *28*
- pumas, *26–27, 28*
- steer skull, *32*

ash (white) wood, 12

B

bears, *18, 27*
bird and waterfowl patterns, *33–37*. *See also* eagle and scroll patterns
- Canada goose, *36*
- canvasback, *37*
- fox and pheasant, *29*
- gun dog and quail, *33*
- mallards, *34, 36*
- merganser, *37*
- pheasants, *29, 35*
- pintail and bobcat, *30*
- quail, *33*

blanks, 10–11
blueprints, checkering, *77–91*
bobcat and pintail, *30*
buffalo, *25, 31*
butt end patterns, *51–53*

C

Canada goose, *36*
canvasback, *37*
carving basics. *See also* patterns; wood
- finishing techniques, 16
- getting started, 10–11
- kits and, 10, 11
- knowing gun's purpose, 7
- practicing first, 13
- skill level, 7
- tool choices, 14–16
- types of carving, 14–16

checkering, 15
checkering blueprints, *77–91*
cherry wood, 12
copying patterns, 8

D

deer patterns, *18–24*
- elk, *24*
- moose, *26*
- mule deer, *19, 21*
- white-tailed deer, *19–20, 21–23*

detail tools, 15
dog and quail, *33*
ducks. *See* bird and waterfowl patterns

E

eagle and scroll patterns, *38–50*
elk, *24*
engraving options, 16

F

figure, wood, 13
files, 15
finishing techniques, 16
fox and pheasant, *29*

G

getting started, 10
goose, *36*
gouges and knives, 14
grade, wood, 13

H

hardwoods, 12
horse, *32*

K

kits, 10, 11
knives and gouges, 14

L

laser engraving, 16

M

mallards, *34, 36*
maple wood, 12
merganser, *37*
moose, *26*
mountain goats and puma, *28*
mule deer, *19, 21*
myrtle wood, 12

P

panel patterns, *54–76*
patterns. *See also* animal patterns
- altering, 8
- butt end, *51–53*
- checkering blueprints, *77–91*
- choosing, 8
- copying, 8
- eagle and scroll, *38–50*
- knowing gun's purpose and, 7
- panel, *54–76*
- relief carving, 14
- restoring guns and, 9
- sizing, 9
- stock templates, *92–94*

pheasants, *29, 35*
pintail and bobcat, *30*
power carving, 15
pumas, *26–27, 28*
purpose, of gun, 7

Q

quail, *33*

R

relief carving, 14
restoring guns, 9

S

sandblasting, 16
scroll and eagle patterns, *38–50*
sizing patterns, 9
skill level, 7
starting out, 10
steer skull, *32*
stock templates, *92–94*

T

tools, 14–16

W

walnut wood, 12
white ash wood, 12
white-tailed deer, *19–20, 21–23*
wood
- blanks, 10–11
- choices/species, 12–13
- figure and grading, 13
- plain-sawn, 13
- practicing on, 13
- quartersawn, 13
- rare, 12
- through-and-through, 13

woodburning, 16

Acknowledgements

The publisher would like to thank the following individuals and companies for providing photos and information to help create this book.

Lora S. Irish/Art Designs Studios
CarvingPatterns.com
LSIrish.com (blog)

Cecil Fredi
702-382-8470
www.gunstockblanks.com
cecil@gunstockblanks.com

Eric M. Saperstein
Artisans of the Valley
Hand Crafted Custom Woodworking
609-637-0450
woodworkers@artisansofthevalley.com
www.artisansofthevalley.com

Gunstock Carving by Bill Janney
937-787-4836
www.billjanney.com
billjanney@billjanney.com

Old Tree Gun Blanks, Inc.
435-669-3901
www.oldtreegunblanks.com
gordon@oldtreegunblanks.com

Track of the Wolf, Inc.
763-633-2500
www.trackofthewolf.com
avid@trackofthewolf.com

West Virginia Wood Arts
304-267-3446
www.westvirginiawoodarts.com

White Creek Gunstock Blanks, LLC
541-597-2118
www.whitecreekgunstockblanks.org
whitecrkgunstock@aol.com

Wood Carvers Supply, Inc.
1-800-284-6229
www.woodcarverssupply.com
teamwcs@yahoo.com

Acquisition editor:
Alan Giagnocavo
Cover and page designer:
Jason Deller
Cover photographer:
Scott Kriner
Developmental editor:
Ayleen Stellhorn
Editor:
Katie Weeber
Layout designer:
Beth Oberholtzer
Proofreader:
Lynda Jo Runkle
Indexer:
Jay Kreider

More Great Books from Fox Chapel Publishing

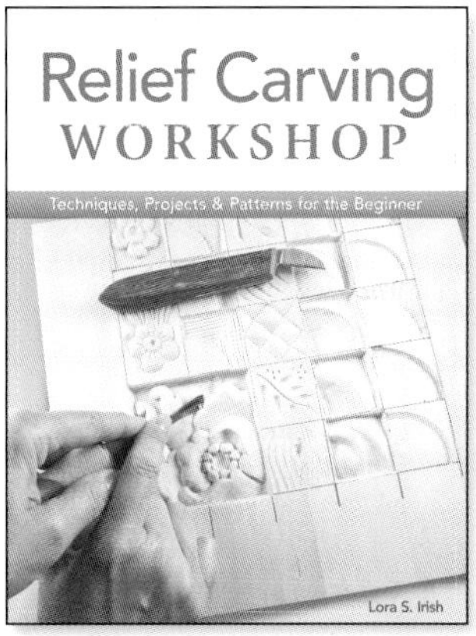

Relief Carving Workshop
ISBN 978-1-56523-736-0 **$19.99**

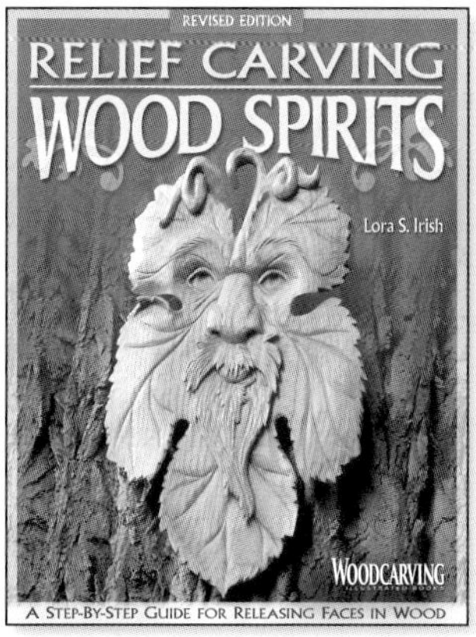

Relief Carving Wood Spirits, Revised Edition
978-1-56523-802-2 **$19.99**

Relief Carving Projects & Techniques
ISBN 978-1-56523-558-8 **$19.95**

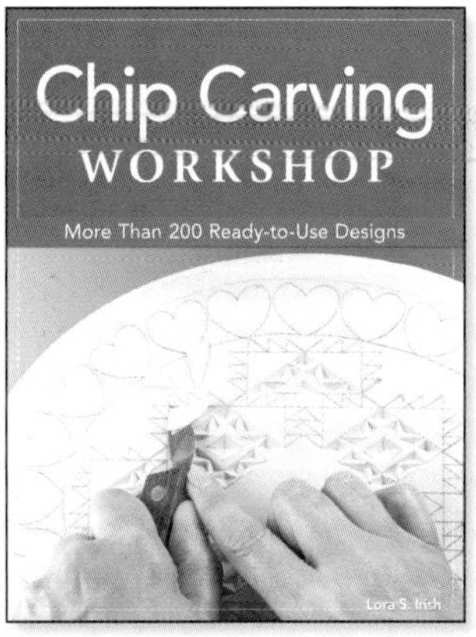

Chip Carving Workshop
ISBN 978-1-56523-776-6 **$16.99**

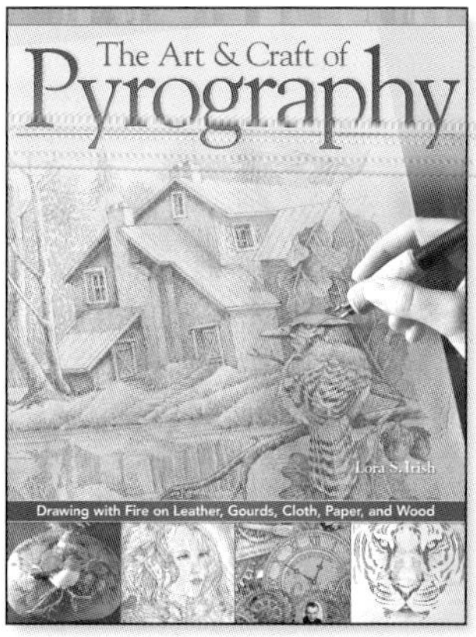

The Art & Craft of Pyrography
ISBN 978-1-56523-478-9 **$19.95**

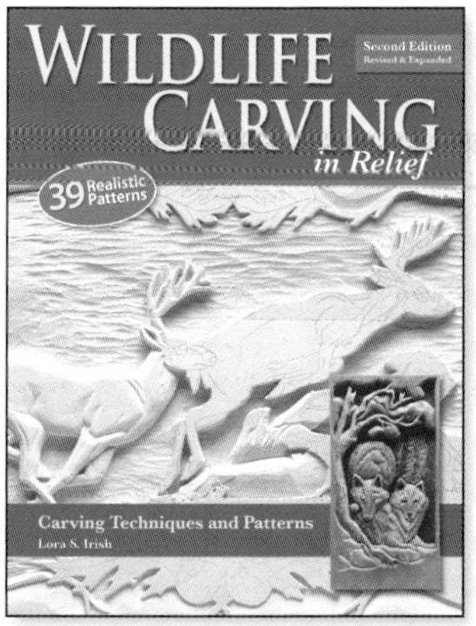

Wildlife Carving in Relief, Second Edition Revised and Expanded
ISBN 978-1-56523-448-2 **$24.95**

WOODCARVING ILLUSTRATED

In addition to being a leading source of woodworking books and DVDs, Fox Chapel also publishes *Woodcarving Illustrated.* Released quarterly, it delivers premium projects, expert tips and techniques from today's finest carvers, and in-depth information about the latest tools, equipment, and materials.

Subscribe Today!
***Woodcarving Illustrated:* 888-506-6630**
www.FoxChapelPublishing.com

Look for These Books at Your Local Bookstore or Specialty Retailer or at *www.FoxChapelPublishing.com*